T0210588

Engaging with Actor-Network Theory as a Methodology in Medical Education Research

This book outlines a methodology based on actor-network theory (ANT) and praxiography and applies this to the field of medical education. Drawn from a detailed account of practice in a medical setting, this book shows how researchers in education and medical education can learn to work with ANT approaches and attune to different insights in practice.

The book gives a detailed account of what actor-network theory can bring to research, through the investigation of social and material networks. The philosophical underpinnings of actor-network theory are presented as the basis of this emerging methodology, through an exploration of learning as disruption, practice as human and material assemblages, and power as regulated difference in worlds of practice. This is a qualitative approach for exploring complexity that does not attempt to represent or reduce but allows for unique insights into practice that might otherwise be overlooked.

With a robust grounding in practice and professional learning and actor-network theory, this book will be of great interest for academics, scholars, and postgraduate students in the field of research methods and medical education.

Bethan Mitchell is Senior Lecturer in Education Studies at the School of Education at Bath Spa University, UK.

Engaging with Actor-Network Theory as a Methodology in Medical Education Research

Bethan Mitchell

Routledge
Taylor & Francis Group

LONDON AND NEW YORK

First published 2021
by Routledge
2 Park Square, Milton Park, Abingdon, Oxon OX14 4RN

and by Routledge
52 Vanderbilt Avenue, New York, NY 10017

Routledge is an imprint of the Taylor & Francis Group, an informa business

British Library Cataloguing-in-Publication Data
A catalogue record for this book is available from the British Library

Library of Congress Cataloging-in-Publication Data
A catalog record for this book has been requested

ISBN: 978-0-367-33224-2 (hbk)
ISBN: 978-0-367-74082-5 (pbk)
ISBN: 978-0-429-31863-4 (ebk)

Typeset in Bembo
by Apex CoVantage, LLC

Contents

Figures

Preface

This book presents a new actor-network theory (ANT) methodology in education research, specifically medical education. ANT draws from philosophical ideas that require translation to be put into practice. The 'praxiographic' approach is sometimes referred to in ANT studies as a way of conducting ethnographic research, but with a focus on practice rather than culture. This book describes an empirical study that draws from ANT and praxiography to create a methodology for research education in practice. Although this book is not a 'how to' guide, it describes a unique approach drawing from ANT, which is enacted as a methodology throughout an entire empirical study. It will be useful to other researchers in education, medical education, professional studies, and practice learning.

At the time of writing in the spring of 2020, there is a global COVID-19 coronavirus pandemic affecting countries all around the world. The immediate effects of social distancing and isolation have resulted in massive changes in day to day living. These effects include millions of people engaging with completely different material assemblages, disrupting and developing new networks, and operating in new worlds of practice. Although it was not the original intention of this book, ANT could be drawn from as a way of seeing how this situation unfolds. For example, in the UK the role of Personal Protective Equipment has become an 'Obligatory Point of Passage' for the treatment of infected patients. ANT is about attuning to what and how things are done rather than what things are, and there is particular value in this approach in the present situation.

Introduction

This book is based on research that was conducted in a hospital setting in the UK. It follows a new approach to studying learning in a workplace setting. The purpose of this book is to put forward how learning can be reconfigured in a workplace setting, and how actor–network theory (ANT) could be drawn from to articulate learning practices. The book describes a specific methodology drawing from three ANT dimensions: networks, symmetry, and multiple worlds. The research presents two study cohorts, from which a selection of anecdotes are analysed using each of the dimensions to illustrate ANT as a sensibility. The methodology develops the idea of 'praxiography' (Mol, 2002) as a way to study practice. The methodology is intended to help other researchers to create their own approaches in ANT and education, rather than to be considered as a set of steps. The examples used to illustrate the methodology are drawn from the original research, which was carried out in a medical education setting, following two teams of medical and pharmacy students as they conducted Student-Led Improvement Science Projects (SLISPs). The methodology described in this book is intended to help education researchers from a range of different fields, as well as medical education.

Structure of the book

Chapter 1: 'ANT as methodology' describes an empirical research study using ANT and praxiography. The chapter introduces the specific methodology developed from the research, drawing from ANT theory and a brand of ethnography designed to focus on practice – praxiography. The ANT dimensions of networks, symmetry, and multiple worlds are presented, which were followed to create a methodological strategy that allowed the researcher to sensitise to relations and effects, rather than people and objects. The rationale for this approach is described in the context of close-to-practice education research, and medical education research. The purpose of the chapter is to describe how the process was followed and how this can be applied to future studies.

The background and history of ANT is outlined in Chapter 2, drawing out particular aspects that are relevant to the empirical research. A number of ideas from ANT are presented, with a focus on the three dimensions of networks, symmetry, and multiple worlds, which are carried through the methodology. This will help readers to conceptualise ANT as a methodological approach rather than a purely theoretical one. There is an overview of current debates and critiques of ANT in the scholarly field in terms of how it is situated and how it has been received.

Chapter 3 presents some of the background information to the empirical study and develops the ideas leading to socio-material conceptualisations of learning in ANT. The background includes improvement science, student-led improvement science projects (referred to in this book as 'SLISP's), and the medical and pharmaceutical practices that students undertake on a hospital ward. This will help the reader to better understand the research setting. It is necessary to provide some of the detail in order to appreciate the setting for the research, particularly if the reader is unfamiliar with the clinical workplace. There is an exploration of the oxymoronic complexities of carrying out an empirical project with students (humans!), whilst at the same time adopting a methodological stance that de-centres the human. The implications of this are explored through professional and practice learning.

Chapter 4 introduces the 'research assemblage' as an ANT methodological strategy. This brings together the concepts described in previous chapters and describes the research as it unfolded. This chapter draws from examples from field-note observations, interviews, reflective notes, and visual analysis of photographs and documents, to show how these were incorporated as a praxiographic approach. The chapter also highlights some of the tensions around using ANT language, sensitising to relations and effects, and how these were reconciled to the idea of 'moving' the data to draw insights, rather than reducing complexity.

Chapters 5 and 6 present the research as a series of anecdotes that were drawn from fieldwork observations, reflections and interviews. Chapter 5 focuses on the ANT research of SLISPs. In the first SLISP, a medical student led a project investigating antimicrobial prescribing. The second SLISP comprised a group of medical and pharmacy students with their project to improve insulin recording. The SLISPs were explored by drawing from three ANT dimensions of networks, symmetry, and multiple worlds. Chapter 6 continues the investigation of improvement science practices, with a particular focus on the pedagogies of improvement science, drawing from professional and practice learning. Through the idea of networks, learning is explored as disruption that occurs as networks collide, picking up and extending Nespor's (2014) *Knowledge in Motion*. Symmetry acknowledges situations as relational, which assists in the refocusing on practice and away from human agency. Finally the notion of multiple worlds, following Law (2004) and Mol (2002), allows for the exploration of how these realities coexist or compete in work-place situations.

In Chapter 7, I speculate as to how this empirical ANT study will help educa-tion researchers in the future, both in wider education and specialist areas such as medical education. Here I extend the work of Bleakley (2012) by adding a practical example to his theoretical explorations of ANT in medical edu-cation, and extend some of the implications put forward by Nespor (2014) and Sørensen (2009) for ANT in education research, and Mol (2002), Law and Singleton (2000) for ANT in healthcare research. I connect with BERA's close-to-practice statement and BMJ's Open Letter (Greenhalgh et al., 2016) to provide a rationale for future research following this methodological approach. Where appropriate, I suggest how the current situation with COVID-19 could be better understood by drawing from an ANT perspective. Five key points are drawn from the research to describe how ANT configures learning. These are: (1) learning can be conceptualised as a network effect. In other words, learn-ing is not restricted to the individual but can be thought of in terms of space/ time. Networks can strengthen, stabilise, and mutate. New networks interact with existing networks, creating effects of destabilisation, change, and learning; (2) material configurations, such as paperwork, stationery, furniture, and so on, shape practice and learning. Humans and non-humans assemble into networks and create effects. By focusing on the relational effects and not the entities themselves, it is possible to conceptualise a situation without privileging the human. In doing so, new insights are brought into focus; (3) workplace projects can enable participants to un-black-box practices by noticing activities that have become taken for granted. Learning emerges as a consequence of changing a 'matter of fact' into a 'matter of concern'. In other words, sets of activities and mundane practices can be made visible; (4) it is possible for learning to emerge through ambiguity and confusion as this can indicate multiple meanings in dif-ferent worlds. In other words, doubts about something which is presented as a singularity can signpost to something more complex. Different versions can co-exist through regulating difference. For example, multiple meanings can be brought together and narrated as a singularity. Alternatively, multiple worlds can exist in incommensurable realities that either co-exist or compete until one is taken over by the other; (5) ordering and assembling of heterogeneous entities can lead to new notions of professionalism. For inter-disciplinary working, team working and collaborative working, new assemblages create new conditions of possibility. In terms of improvement science, new ways of working can challenge membership of professional groups, leading to new groupings and possibilities.

Chapter 8 describes what this empirical project taught me about approaches in the field, and what I achieved and fell short of. There are personal anec-dotes that helped me to understand the process. This was a strong part of my research, and future researchers might find it helpful to know what went on behind the scenes, and the effort that went in to developing the approach.

References

Bleakley, A. (2012). The proof is in the pudding: Putting actor-network-theory to work in medical education. *Medical Teacher*, 34(6), pp. 462–467.

Greenhalgh, T., Annandale, E., Ashcroft, R., Barlow, J., Black, N., Bleakley, A., Boaden, R., Braithwaite, J., Britten, N. and Carnevale, F. (2016). An open letter to The BMJ editors on qualitative research. *BMJ*, 352 (i563).

Law, J. (2004). *After method: Mess in social science research*. London: Routledge.

Law, J. and Singleton, V. (2000). *This is not an object*. Lancaster: Centre for Science Studies, Lancaster University. Available at: http://www.comp.lancs.ac.uk/sociology/papers/Law-Singleton-This-is-Not-an-Object.pdf. Last accessed on 15th November 2017.

Mol, A. (2002). *The body multiple: Ontology in medical practice*. Durham: Duke University Press.

Nespor, J. (2014). *Knowledge in motion: Space, time and curriculum in undergraduate physics and management*. Abingdon: Routledge.

Sørensen, E. (2009). *The materiality of learning: Technology and knowledge in educational practice*. Cambridge: Cambridge University Press.

Chapter 1

ANT as methodology

This chapter sets the tone for actor–network theory (ANT) as methodology and presents the background to the research described in this book. It introduces improvement science as an innovative approach currently being applied in hospitals, and describes other studies that have contributed to the exploration of this approach. The research followed two Student-Led Improvement Science Projects (SLISPs) in the setting of hospital wards. ANT is situated as a methodology for the research, drawing from the key principles of networks, symmetry, and multiple worlds. The chapter briefly describes some of the stories that arose from the findings, which draw from these principles. Praxiography is presented as the overarching method for the fieldwork. As the research unfolds, ANT enables new configurations and readings of how learning emerges through practice in medical education, which can be related to the current situation with COVID-19.

Background to the research

Skin marks the boundary of the patient's body, but paperwork and numbers extend it; parts of the patient (blood, samples) are extracted and sent to labs. Tubes (cannulas, catheters) are inserted into the patient's body, set on metal poles from which the patient can't extricate themselves. Patients are placed in cubicles in bays or in side rooms. They are prone, or move slowly, while practitioners move purposefully around them. They are identified by their pyjamas, their position, their movement (or lack of it). The patient is a network, connected to paper, numbers, plastic and metal, position, time. The patient's body is in the bed all the time, night and day. The staff come and go: this is their work.

Paperwork is bounded in files: plastic ring-binders, paper manila folders, or clasped together on a clipboard; attached by holes or pressure; stuck with tape or sticky paper. Marked – inscribed – by pen in different hands: different pen, different styles of writing, text and symbols. The ring-binders are in the bay, the patients' bodies are in the beds. Everything has its place in the ward. The paperwork recording the patient's 'antibiotic story' is messy, full of codes and cues. Protocol is interpreted and weighed up alongside other activities that require different materials, objects, different types of paper. The hidden: lab results, sensitivity and resistance, a plethora of available drugs (some of which have more power that others; the preference to use vancomycin to gentamycin because the latter is considered to be more risky, harmful, fiddly, too many stipulations) with mysterious names. Other treatments that aren't antibiotics confuse the story: painkillers, anti-inflammatories; timings of medicine dispensing, timescales dictated by the gentamycin chart and arrival of lab results. Or – in the middle of the night – is the patient asleep, can they swallow?

A sign in the doctor's adjoining room says: 'Please return the files to the trolley': the files are picked up and handled frequently, marked inside and out. For the ward round, the trolleys are moved around by the doctors. Staff crowd around some notes – humans and non-humans assembling. Staff crowd around the patient, around the Specialist Registrar like a Higgs Boson, forces pulling. Wait for the telephone to ring with results – creatine levels to prescribe the next dose of gentamycin in the correct timeframe. Foundation Year doctors access particular PCs with the software to calculate doses. They sign the form to instruct the nurse to administer – wait for the nurse to do the rounds: intra-venous or oral? The materiality assembled by this decision impacts on the nurse's work, the patient's comfort (can the patient swallow? Can the nurse find a vein for the cannula?), the rapidity of the antibiotic into the system, levels of toxicity, the chart, the calculation, the written dose, the signature, the notes: part of the patient, part of the network.

Networks of relations strengthen or weaken, break and mutate. The diagnosed condition of the patient becomes multiple, a cluster of numbers and names on different pieces of paper, attached in different files and clipped on boards. The patient has a 'history', but it's not clear how far to go back. The history is segmented into files, electronic and paper-based, in different places and on different forms, different handwriting, different concerns. The nurses need to know X, the doctors, Y, sometimes they need to know the same thing for different reasons. The decision for the patient, for their treatment, translated in the power of the inscription of the result, in the experience and command that assembles.

The above description, a reflective piece that was written after attending an observation, does not directly answer any questions or provide any solutions; it describes a workplace scenario. The approach in this book is to attend to the particular, to appreciate and explore, to draw out relations and associations. Describing the entanglements of entities, the way they come together and the effects these produce, draws attention to minute practices and mundane realities that might otherwise be overlooked. In the scenario described, the material and the social are presented equally, with no attempt to ascribe agency or motivation to specific actors. Again, this shifts attention to places and practices that become taken-for-granted, things that slip through the net of research. This book argues that, to appreciate the workplace from an education perspective, to trace learning and knowledge as effects produced from interactions in space/time, it is necessary to adopt an approach that allows new and challenging descriptions to emerge.

Medical education in the NHS in the UK has a focus on inter-professional working and collaboration to achieve more 'patient-centred care', and values are being reoriented away from the individual and towards the collective (Bleakley, 2014). This change, coupled with government demands for more 'efficient and cost-effective' work processes (The Evidence Centre, 2011), has culminated in the need for clinical staff across disciplines to engage with quality improvement in the workplace, and for consistent approaches to implement change. As Dahlgren and colleagues (2012, p. 186) argue, 'Quality in health care is ultimately about the patients' health and life and, it is argued, is dependent on collaboration between different actors in the health-care system, professionals, future professionals, patients and families'. To address these demands, the NHS has adopted improvement methods from other sectors, such as aviation and manufacturing (Worrall, 2008). One such measure that has been taken up recently in the NHS is improvement science. The changing nature of professionalism arising from these measures creates new learning requirements but also new tensions, such as the instability that interrupts consistent and established work practices (Fenwick and Nerland, 2014), and unintended consequences which may have repercussions in risk and safety. In addition, the values and ethos of private sector practices espoused by improvement science and originating from manufacturing is rooted in profit and turnover, and promotes managerialist approaches, which can be at odds with public sector healthcare (Turbitt, Mathias and de Jong, 2010).

'Improvement science' was considered to be an appropriate subject for research because of the salience and increasing attention brought to its application in hospitals and other workplaces. At the time that the research was being conducted, improvement science was becoming part of the discourse of quality improvement in the NHS to promote staff-led, localised improvements, with a standardised approach (The Evidence Centre, 2011). The approach incorporates methods such as Plan, Do, Study, Act (PDSA) cycles, where a change is tested at different stages, run charts, process modelling, and problem-solving diagrams. SLISPs adopted these approaches in hospitals in the UK. The introduction of improvement science into learning programmes requires students to learn a set of strategies and approaches relating to the identification, implementation, and management of improvements in the workplace (The Institute for Healthcare Improvement, 2015). It is not the intention of this book to investigate the effectiveness of improvement science or the changes it brings about to organisations. Rather, the purpose is to present a new methodology that traces the fine-grained activities, materials, spaces, behaviours, and relationships that emerge during workplace projects, and how learning can be reconfigured and articulated by drawing from ANT.

The introduction of improvement science to medical education, discussed in Chapter 3, presents opportunities to explore different pedagogies and to reconfigure learning for students. In the research described in this book, the students come from medical and pharmacy backgrounds. In the UK, medicine and pharmacy are two disparate disciplines, accountable to different bodies (Royal College of Physicians (RCP) and General Medical Council (GMC) for medicine; Association of the British Pharmaceutical Industry (ABPI) and General Pharmaceutical Council (GPhC) for pharmacy). The inclusion of different disciplines is relevant to this research because of the growing emphasis on inter-professional practice and learning (Bleakley, Bligh and Browne, 2011; Bleakley, 2012, 2014). For medical students, the standards in Tomorrow's Doctors include working and learning in a multi-professional team to improve patient care professionalism. The standards of professionalism also comprise clinical, ethical, legal, and moral responsibilities alongside respect, politeness, consideration, and trustworthiness (General Medical Council Education Committee, 1993). Alongside these developments towards inter-professional and team-based learning is a tradition of individualised working. Historically, the Flexner Report of 1910 promoted the 'character' of the 'good doctor', encouraging a particular idea of what doctors should be (Kuper, Whitehead and Hodges, 2013; Whitehead, Hodges and Austin, 2013) and has led to the perception of the heroic individual (Bleakley, Bligh and Browne, 2011). The transition to more collective ways of working signals a shift in culture, requiring different learning and working methods. Simulation is one such approach that is becoming more widely used in medicine and pharmacy (Ahn et al., 2015; Buchan et al., 2014) as a way of practicing in clinical teams (Bleakley, 2014). Medical students also have the opportunity to engage in workplace learning on the hospital ward (Paterson et al., 2011). Workplace learning is considered to be advantageous for medical students by focusing on the integration of practical and emotional learning (Dornan, Scherpbier and Boshuizen, 2009). There is also research that demonstrates the potential advantages of having students present in clinical settings; some report transformative learning for both the experienced healthcare professional and the student (Grant et al., 2010).

Actor-network theory and researching learning

The term 'Student-led Improvement Science Projects' (SLISPs) was created for this study to describe the combination of student project leadership and the application of improvement science methods. Two teams of medical and pharmacy students were studied as they undertook their projects, set on hospital wards. The questions raised at the start of the research were: How is learning configured when carrying out improvement science projects? How do we conceptualise learning for medical students moving beyond individualised learning, and what new insights could this bring to medical education and education in general? The result of the study and analysis is a new ANT methodology, from which researchers in education and medical education can learn to work with ANT approaches and attune to different insights in practice that might otherwise be overlooked.

ANT, as an approach that encourages a focus on nuance and minutiae, has been drawn from in this research to explore how professional learning is enacted during the process of a SLISP. In current research, evaluations of improvement science projects have been conducted as clinical projects (Armstrong, Lauder and Shepherd, 2015; James et al., 2016), and ANT has been applied to medical education in medical simulation (Ahn et al., 2015). This research is the first exploration of improvement science projects through the lens of ANT. This research addresses this gap and puts forward a new way of investigating improvement science projects in medical education, as well as developing ANT as a methodology. This provides broader possibilities for pedagogies of improvement science and offers new ways to conceptualise the position of students as project leaders and agents of change in workplace practice. ANT is particularly suited to this type of investigation, and provides a way of articulating how humans and non-humans assemble to form networks of practices that might otherwise be overlooked (Latour and Woolgar, 2013). In summary, there is a general movement in medical education towards more collaborative ways of learning. Bleakley, Bligh and Browne (2011) argue that this requires taking on theories, such as ANT, which can provide a language of learning other than individual and acquisitional. The SLISPs also require pedagogic approaches that accommodate working in inter-disciplinary groups, with clinical teams and in a clinical setting.

This book describes how the research explored learning that emerges as medical and pharmacy students carry out SLISPs. The aim was to trace the fine-grained activities, materials, spaces, behaviours, and relationships that emerged during projects, with the purpose of gaining a better understanding of how learning and knowledge emerge as network effects. This book focuses on what the ANT concepts of networks, symmetry, and multiple worlds bring to medical education and education in general. A number of questions guided the research, ultimately working towards an ANT methodology that could be drawn from in future research. These were based on the three ANT dimensions of networks, symmetry, and multiple worlds. From the dimension of networks, the research explored how networks assembled, what work was holding the network in place through connections, the nature of these connections as weak, strong, temporary, and so on, and the effects that emerged. From the symmetry dimension, the research explored how spatial and temporal arrangements restrict or facilitate possibilities for learning, and how materials invite, exclude, or regulate practice. The dimension of multiple worlds describes how different worlds coexist or dominate another in the same practices, and asks the question: what is at stake? In other words, what is sacrificed by making the decision to choose one version over another?

ANT, as a socio-material approach, addresses paradigmatic controversies (Lincoln, Lynham and Guba, 2011) by challenging the way in which the social and material have come to be separated (Latour, 2012). Although the study is not a direct critique or evaluation, ANT enables the scientism of improvement science to be challenged. Part of the motivation for my research and adoption of ANT is that in order to assess learning in SLISPs, it is first necessary to understand the value of that learning and how it is enacted. For example, if SLISPs are contributing to assessment for grading, there needs to be a better understanding of what they are through what they do; ANT is a method that gives a detailed description of practice and how practice shapes reality and the people that are enrolled in it (Law, 2004). The reason for my decision to draw from ANT is because of its fluidity and flexibility, which enables it to be adapted to contexts rather than forcing the cases into predefined methodological boxes. This divergent approach might be termed 'untriangulation', as Bleakley (2012) positions ANT as the opposite of triangulation. As illustrated in the next chapter, ANT enables the researcher to trouble the notion of privileging the human, and hence the position of students as change agents. ANT attunes to what is often overlooked (Latour and Woolgar, 2013), and to relations; the focus is on what things do rather than what things mean (Fenwick and Edwards, 2010; Latour, 2005). Because of this, my research illustrates how potentially overlooked factors, such as the colour of a sticker on a form, may be critical in stabilising or destabilising networks of practice and learning. It also shows how decisions that appear to be made about such factors emerge in a process that is distributed over space and time, between actors that include material objects as well as the ones who are nominally 'leading' the improvement. The ANT concept of multiple worlds provides a language to unfold practice and learning, and to trouble the idea of improvement science as a singularity into a multiple.

The research story

In considering the main 'characters' from the research, I was first drawn to introduce the students who might be termed the 'research subjects'. However, this presents a dilemma. One of the central principles of ANT is that of 'symmetry'. Symmetry enables a way of seeing the world without putting humans and human action at the centre. The reason for this is to notice interactions and connections in practice without paying too much attention to what we assume to be most important. In having the students as central actors, I am going against the grain of ANT by attaching more importance to humans than non-humans. So rather than introduce human characters it might be helpful to consider this: a human is a network of human and non-human entities that have assembled together. A person is a network and is part of a network. Like the description at the start of this chapter, a patient can be considered embodied and dispersed through inscriptions and records, samples, cannulas, medicines, beds, and corridors. Similarly, the researcher can be considered as part of a network of supervisors, colleagues, publications, presentations, wide-eyed wonder, and naïve speculation. Rather than have one person at the forefront of the network, shift the position and an object comes into view. Shift again and the connections and links become evident. This is a story of noticing networks and assemblages, to consider new conditions of possibility that occur when we are no longer distracted by our own assumptions.

The story of the locker

Later on, I introduce the story (anecdote) of the locker. Before I start telling the story, I want to emphasise the research orientation in education research. This is a research story about learning. I could have written a research story about what the medical and pharmacy students learned when they carried out improvement science projects. I could have interviewed the students before and after the project, asking directly: 'What did you learn?' However, the aim of my research was to reconceptualise learning as socio-material, enacted in practices as an effect, rather than as a human phenomenon. To achieve this I attended to materials, what I observed around me, how they came together to form a network. One object that came to my attention was the locker.

The locker was situated in a locker room with a keypad on the door. The correct code was needed to enter the room. Once inside, rows of lockers housed items considered valuable, or at least valuable enough for the owners to wish to be reunited with them. I was introduced to the locker by the medical student in my second cohort. Generously, the medical student offered its use to the two pharmacy students in their team. This required the use of a key. My second cohort conducted their project largely online, employing an array of software and equipment. One software platform, Slack, was used for communications on and off site, and was used to send messages regarding the location of the key. Slack was available on an app, and the students accessed the app through phones, iPads, and laptops. However, the purpose of the locker was to store iPads and laptops. Hence, a network formed around the complex interactions between humans and materials that affected the execution of the project. It would be simple to say that the students had agency, that they controlled the project. It is more of a challenge to see this from the locker in a central position, as a site of power and as an influencer of learning. This was my challenge.

In the following chapters, ANT is presented as a practical and working theory (although ANT is not a theory, as we discover later). ANT as methodology might not unfurl in expected ways; it does not strive for the rigidity of a framework or the utility of a tool. What I offer in the following chapters is the story of my own research and how ANT formed part of this network. I am sure there are plot-holes and loose ends. But I would ask you, the reader, to follow Latour when he said: 'Be not the one who debunks, but the one who assembles' (Latour, 2004).

Praxiography as researching practice

The core of the book describes a particular piece of research through the lens of ANT. ANT provides a way of seeing the detail of situations, and draws out connections and relations. ANT is one of a number of approaches that considers the material alongside the social. In education, this enables detailed descriptions of how practices are enacted. In traditional readings of education, learning and knowledge are essentialised, that is, presented as objectified 'things' that can grow, be acquired, and be measured. In some cases, this is restrictive, and can limit the possibilities of what learning and knowledge could be. Thinking of learning and knowledge as collective and social, rather than something that happens to individuals, can create new ways of seeing education in practice. Extending these ideas to include the material can take ideas even further.

For my research, I followed the work of Latour and Woolgar (2013), Nespor (2014) and Sørensen (2009) for their descriptions of networks and how these were presented empirically. Latour and Woolgar (2013) described an ethnography they had undertaken in order to describe laboratory practices from an outsider's perspective. It was interesting how they described some of the activities in terms of how people and things were connected, rather than falling back on assumptions that laboratory technicians might use themselves. For example, a laboratory technician might say that they were titrating, but Latour and Woolgar would say that they were working on a bench with glassware, reaching up to manipulate the tap whilst at the same time turning a flask in a circular motion to catch the liquid. This is significant, as the laboratory technicians in the book had 'black-boxed' practices they were used to, instead of considering all the steps, configurations, and possibilities. Nespor's (2014) research was orientated directly in education practices. This research presented learning as a network effect by describing the practices and assemblages that made up two very different types of undergraduate course. By studying the practices of a management course and a physics course, Nespor (2014) was able to describe learning as circulating and moving through the interactions and connections that were created for each course. Sørensen's (2009) research was also situated in education, and described how learning could be considered as part of network activities.

Following other empirical ANT studies of learning, I found that the network metaphor helped me to navigate through my fieldwork and analysis, but I felt that more could be drawn from ANT. Much had been written about the concept of symmetry in ANT, especially in the critiques, and I felt this needed to be addressed as a perspective in my research. Symmetry can be difficult to write about, especially in terms of presenting non-human entities on an equal footing to humans. Some of the dilemmas surrounding this are discussed in later chapters. The movement 'After ANT' prompted thinking around the way socio-materiality shapes practice and reality. In the research described in this book, I draw from the notion of multiple worlds to explore socio-material readings of learning.

I first described my methodological approach as ethnography, as I was immersed in the activities of the SLISP, and observing what was going on around me. However, ethnography is derived from anthropology, and is focused on the human. As I was following an ANT sensibility, I wanted to attune to the material, and not to foreground the human as the central actant. Mol (2002) presents praxiography as an approach to researching situations with a focus on practice, on the relational and connected enactments that take place, rather than the actants themselves. This also draws attention to local variations rather than universal generalisations, hence an object in one place may not behave the same way in another. Although this might seem at odds to 'follow the actor', I used this technique to attune to connections rather than to focus on the actant itself.

A note on COVID-19

The description at the start of this chapter is particularly poignant in March 2020, at the time of writing. Currently, the news is filled with images of hospital wards, with medical staff covered head to toe in blue gowns, visors, facemasks, and gloves. The materiality of the clinical setting is even more prominent. News stories abound about ventilators, oxygen, beds and spaces for patients, and buildings converted to morgues. It becomes more feasible to imagine a human as a network of materials that connect, as an assemblage of heterogeneous entities that are drawn together. Life and death rely on PPE and ventilators and of setting a spatial distance, the length that a droplet can spray and cause infection, and of repellent fabric that avoids transference of virus-laden fluids. Attending to relational materiality in this situation may help future researchers notice practices that might otherwise be overlooked.

References

Ahn, S., Rimpiläinen, S., Theodorsson, A., Fenwick, T. and Dahlgren, M.A. (2015). Learning in technology-enhanced medical simulation: Locations and knowings. *Professions and Professionalism*, 5(3).

Armstrong, L., Lauder, W. and Shepherd, A. (2015). An evaluation of methods used to teach quality improvement to undergraduate healthcare students to inform curriculum development within preregistration nurse education: A protocol for systematic review and narrative synthesis. *Systematic Reviews*, 4(1), p. 8.

Bleakley, A. (2012). The proof is in the pudding: Putting actor-network-theory to work in medical education. *Medical Teacher*, 34(6), pp. 462–467.

Bleakley, A. (2014). *Patient-centred medicine in transition: The heart of the matter*. Vol. 3. Heidelberg: Springer Science & Business Media.

Bleakley, A., Bligh, J. and Browne, J. (2011). *Medical education for the future: Identity, power and location*. Heidelberg: Springer Science & Business Media.

Buchan, S., Regan, K., Filion-Murphy, C., Little, K., Strath, A., Rowe, I. and Vosper, H. (2014). Students as partners in a quality improvement approach to learning enhancement: A case study from a pharmacy undergraduate course. *Communicare*, 1(1).

Dahlgren, M.A., Dahlgren, L.O. and Dahlberg, J. (2012). Learning professional practice through education. In: P. Hager, A. Lee and A. Reich, eds., *Practice, learning and change: Practice-theory perspectives on professional learning*. Dordrecht: Springer, pp. 183–197.

Dornan, T., Scherpbier, A. and Boshuizen, H. (2009). Supporting medical students' workplace learning: Experience-based learning (ExBL). *The Clinical Teacher*, 6(3), pp. 167–171.

The Evidence Centre. (2011). *Evidence scan: Improvement science.* London: The Health Foundation. Available at: www.health.org.uk/sites/health/files/Improvement Science.pdf [Accessed 11 Nov. 2017].

General Medical Council Education Committee. (1993). *Tomorrow's doctors: Recommendations on undergraduate medical education.* London: General Medical Council.

Grant, A., Prout, H., Hawthorne, K., Jones, T.L. and Houston, H. (2010). Some effects of teaching undergraduate medical students on general practitioner thinking and learning. *Education for Primary Care,* 21(2), pp. 97–104.

Fenwick, T. and Edwards, R. (2010). *Actor-network theory in education.* London: Routledge.

Fenwick, T. and Nerland, M. (2014). *Reconceptualising professional learning: Sociomaterial knowledges, practices and responsibilities.* Abingdon: Routledge.

The Institute for Healthcare Improvement. (2015). *Initiatives: Scottish patient safety programme.* Available at: www.ihi.org/Engage/Initiatives/Completed/ScottishPatientSafety/Pages/default.aspx [Accessed 11 Nov. 2017].

James, B., Beattie, M., Shepherd, A., Armstrong, L. and Wilkinson, J. (2016). Time, fear and transformation: Student nurses' experiences of doing a practicum (quality improvement project) in practice. *Nurse Education in Practice,* 19, pp. 70–78.

Kuper, A., Whitehead, C. and Hodges, B.D. (2013). Looking back to move forward: Using history, discourse and text in medical education research: AMEE Guide No. 73. *Medical Teacher,* 35(1), pp. e849–e860.

Latour, B. (2004). Why has critique run out of steam? From matters of fact to matters of concern. *Critical Inquiry,* 30(2), pp. 225–248.

Latour, B. (2005). *Reassembling the social: An introduction to actor-network-theory.* Oxford: Oxford University Press.

Latour, B. (2012). *We have never been modern.* Cambridge, MA: Harvard University Press.

Latour, B. and Woolgar, S. (2013). *Laboratory life: The construction of scientific facts.* Princeton, NJ: Princeton University Press.

Law, J. (2004). *After method: Mess in social science research.* London: Routledge.

Lincoln, Y.S., Lynham, S.A. and Guba, E.G. (2011). Paradigmatic controversies, contradictions, and emerging confluences, revisited. In: N.K. Denzin and Y.S. Lincoln, eds., *The Sage handbook of qualitative research.* 4th ed. London: Sage, pp. 97–128.

Mol, A. (2002). *The body multiple: Ontology in medical practice.* Durham: Duke University Press.

Nespor, J. (2014). *Knowledge in motion: Space, time and curriculum in undergraduate physics and management.* Abingdon: Routledge.

Sørensen, E. (2009). *The materiality of learning: Technology and knowledge in educational practice.* Cambridge: Cambridge University Press.

Turbitt, I., Mathias, M. and de Jong, J. (2010). The Kafka brigade: Public management theory in practice. Kafka Brigade paper, *Winelands Conference* 2010, File 2. DOI: 10.13140/RG.2.1.2304.4329.

Whitehead, C.R., Hodges, B.D. and Austin, Z. (2013). Dissecting the doctor: From character to characteristics in North American medical education. *Advances in Health Sciences Education,* 18(4), pp. 687–699.

Worrall, M. (2008). Chocks away? Time for a surgical checklist. *The Bulletin of the Royal College of Surgeons of England,* 90(9), pp. 304–305.

Chapter 2

A brief history of ANT

This chapter introduces ANT as a socio-material approach in education. Early, or classic, ANT ideas are outlined, focusing on networks and how these are explored in education research literature and seminal works that have influenced this research. The notion of symmetry is then explored in relation to networks and other ANT principles. Critiques, particularly focusing on symmetry, are introduced and presented. The chapter then moves into a discussion of 'after-ANT' and multiple worlds (Law and Hassard, 1999) and of tensions in this field, both theoretical and practical. Finally, the chapter explores ANT in practice, and how language needs to be considered in ANT descriptions.

The umbrella term of socio-materiality

In education research, ANT is included under the umbrella term of socio-materiality. The socio-material brings materials back into research, rather than solely focusing on humans, which helps researchers explore practice and find new ways of attuning to situations. Socio-materiality is becoming more broadly talked about in medical education (Falk, Hopwood, and Dahlgren, 2017; Fenwick, 2014; Goldszmidt and Faden, 2016; McMurtry, Rohse and Kilgour, 2016), with some studies focusing specifically on ANT in clinical practice, for example, surgical skills (Ibrahim, Richardson and Nestel, 2015). Fenwick, Edwards, and Sawchuk (2011) include complexity theory, cultural historical activity theory (CHAT), ANT, and spatiality theories within this term. Fenwick, Edwards and Sawchuk (2011) identify four commonalities that connect these theories: they all take on whole systems and the entangled nature of human and non-human action; they trace how bodies (such as bodies of knowledge) are stabilised through activity; and they de-centre the human by flattening hierarchies rather than making some things more important than others. However, it is widely acknowledged that the distinct traditions and histories of each of these approaches also need to be taken into consideration. For example, CHAT has emerged out of Marxist and Vygotskian conceptualisations of systems and learning, and has an established connection with education (Engeström, 2001), whereas ANT has been developed in Science and

Technology Studies (STS) and has been drawn into education (Fenwick and Edwards, 2010; Nespor, 2014; Sørensen, 2009; Verran, 2001). These histories are significant in terms of how concepts have developed over time, with different associations and traditions, and it is necessary to understand this diversity before applying an all-encompassing term such as socio-materiality.

As one of the socio-material approaches, ANT is viewed as more of a sensibility than a theory (Fenwick, Edwards and Sawchuk, 2011), and there are many discussions regarding the status of ANT as a theory. Latour's (2005) argument is that ANT can be considered as a method by which the researchers can learn from the actors without imposing their own views. Mol's (2010) argument is that ANT findings are not synthesised into a framework, and that ANT is not 'applied' in a deterministic or causal manner; empirical studies are considered as a way of developing the approach in a dynamic and fluid way (Law, 2006). A very recent addition to the corpus of ANT theory papers introduces the notion of 'the ANT multiple' (Kanger, 2017). This situates ANT as theory and methodology, presenting seven categories: ANT as an ontological and sensitising framework; ANT as an empirical 'tool' to construct middle-range theory; ANT as analysis; ANT as framework for 'fluid' situations; ANT as guided methodology; ANT as ontological and methodological assumptions; and finally, ANT as undefinable. The implications are that ANT is at a stage where a broad range of studies have amassed in different fields and disciplines, and it would be helpful for future research to attempt to bring these together in some way, although this does not necessitate its culminating into an overarching theory.

Fenwick, Edwards and Sawchuk (2011) argue that ANT is not a theory about learning but is rather a method to understand how effects, such as knowledge, identities, powerful centres, and practices, are produced through assemblages of heterogeneous human and non-human elements. Rather than setting out a defined approach that is imposed onto a research study, ANT is performed into being by the growing number of empirical research studies (Law, 2006).

Actor-network theory: history and overview

There are many ways to present ANT and many concepts and methodological devices to draw from. Part of the appeal and, conversely, the frustration of ANT is that it is constantly being redefined through theoretical discussion and empirical research. This process serves to keep ANT vital but also makes it difficult to 'pin down'. The result is a confusing array of claims and exclusions that sometimes appear coherent, sometimes not. As Law and Hassard proclaim:

> actor-network theory is not something in particular. But then again . . . neither is it simply a random set of bits and pieces, wreckage spread along the hard shoulder of the superhighway of theory.
>
> (Law and Hassard, 1999, p. 10)

The literature conveys ANT as diasporic (Fenwick, Edwards, and Sawchuk, 2011), a collection of accounts (Law, 2006) and as a theory in its loosest sense (Mol, 2010). ANT has been referred to as: the sociology of translation (Brown and Capdevila, 1999), the semiotics of materiality (Law and Hassard, 1999), relational materiality (Law and Hassard, 1999), and actant-rhizome ontology (Lynch in Latour, 1999b). These terms describe some of the facets of ANT as pulling together matter and meaning, and as a way of seeing the world through connections. Although some of these labels perhaps more accurately reflect the approach, the three-letter 'ANT' acronym has endured. Latour (1999b), one of the most prolific and well-known contributors in the field, has criticised the acronym on the basis that 'actor-network' appears to support the agency/ structure debate in the social sciences (which it does not) and 'theory' suggests a causal or predictive model (which it is not). Law (1999) talks about the ANT acronym as 'a sign of replicability. Of its diffusion. Or, perhaps better, of its translation' (Law and Hassard, 1999, p. 2).

ANT has been taken up in many different areas, such as management and organisation studies (e.g. McLean and Hassard, 2004); education (e.g. Fenwick, Nerland and Jensen, 2014); health (e.g. Law and Singleton, 2000; Mol, 2002); and medical education (e.g. Bleakley, Bligh and Browne, 2011). Historically, ANT is rooted in STS. Seminal works are situated in science and engineering, most notably Callon's study of scallop fishing in St Bruic's Bay (Michael, 1996) and Latour's studies of laboratory practices (Latour and Woolgar, 2013). These reflect the development of ANT as an ethnography of scientific practices (Law, 2004b). It is important to note the development of ontological debates in science preceding STS and ANT. For example, Fleck's (1981) *Genesis and Development of a Scientific Fact*, written in 1935, which influenced Kuhn's *Structure of Scientific Revolutions*. The impact of these works is far-reaching, and has presented science and sociology in new ways. For example, Latour and Woolgar (2013) shifted attention from human actors and interests such as cognitive, institutional and cultural foci, and instead drew attention to how heterogenous elements are aligned to produce scientific 'truths' (Michael, 1996). In terms of ontology, ANT is orientated with post-structuralist thinking, where the idea of discovering aspects of external reality is replaced with the idea that reality is in flux (Law, 2004b). Ideas in ANT eschew rigid categories which can shape assumptions (Fenwick and Edwards, 2010). For example, a policy or a species of plant might be given a label and placed into a group that is built on previous ways of categorising, without considering how that policy or species is enacted in practice or the forces and effects it creates, or how it might be associated with other entities. This positions ANT as a relational theory, reflecting 'the view that a thing is defined solely by its effects and alliances rather than by the lonely inner kernel of essence' (Harman, 2010, p. 75). Czarniawska and Hernes (2020) describe how Latour follows on from Greimas' actant theory, where the effect of one subject upon another creates a changed state. In other words, an ANT analysis will explore a situation for its *relations* rather than the intrinsic properties of *entities*; this can be challenging and requires scrutiny of detail to build descriptions of enactment in practice. Law (2004a) relates ANT to the idea of baroque complexity, meaning that ANT has a predilection to look down into the detail of a situation through unfolding description, or Leibnitz's analogy of 'ponds within ponds', rather than looking up at projected patterns and representations of the world. Rather than focusing solely on humans as the agentic actors in the workplace, an ANT study will consider relations and effects between components.

As well as questioning the position of the human, an ANT position challenges established notions of the social as being separate from nature or the material world. ANT thinking diverges from the idea of social constructivism by questioning the social (and human) as the creator of reality. Instead, Latour (1999a) refers to 'circulating reference', where metaphysical reality and constructed reality are not bifurcated but instead become part of the same way of thinking, as an 'enriched version of realism' (Harman, 2010, p. 73). Harman (2010) describes Latour's idea of circulating reference as the ubiquitous translations that occur in the world, rather than modern philosophy's insistence that translations are centred on the point between human and world. This rejection of bifurcations is critical to ANT thinking and is the core of Latour's argument for equal treatment of humans and non-humans. Latour (2012) contends that modernity exacerbated, or purified, a rift between natural science and the social, which influences the way in which we are encouraged to see the world. By perpetuating this split, there is a risk that the social becomes more and more removed from the scientific, creating islands of reality that are explored as separate entities. The implications of this rift are that 'things' such as beetles, earth, buildings, and diseases exist as isolated entities that can be measured, whereas the social constructs its own reality that is entirely separate. ANT affords an alternative ontology, where such dichotomies are challenged and the arbitrary boundaries that have been set up to isolate entities from each other are broken down. Forcing these two worlds back together after (as ANT contends) falsely separating them is problematic because of the ontological differences. Conventional approaches do not currently enable the social and the material to be explored in the same way. An alternative ontology is required which can be found in ANT.

As a methodology, there is no 'correct' way to perform ANT. Unlike many other approaches, there are no set stages for the researcher to follow, and no model to fix on. Law suggests that this is one of the strengths of ANT, as: 'Only dead theories and dead practices seek to reflect, in every detail, the practices which came before' (Law and Hassard, 1999, p. 10).

Three dimensions of ANT

ANT can be described as a set of tenets, principles, and so on. There is coherence to the approach, but this is sometimes difficult to describe in terms of where the boundaries lie. This section concentrates on three 'dimensions' of ANT, networks, symmetry, and multiple worlds, to attempt to pull together early-ANT and after-ANT.

The term 'network' is used to describe an assemblage of human and non-human entities that are held together through continual work to produce identities, environment and knowledge. The concept of networks has endured in ANT and has been the basis of many empirical works. ANT authors refer to the idea of networks as 'classic' ANT (Gorur, 2012; Sørensen, 2009). Classic, or early, ANT refers to the original studies and discussions from STS and the works of Callon and Latour on networks. For example, Callon's principles of translation (Callon, 1984) are a popular approach to studying actor-networks, and have been drawn from in empirical education studies (Nespor, 2014; Zukas and Kilminster, 2014). More latterly, and as part of the movement of after-ANT, networks have been problematised and reimagined to reflect the developments of the use of actor-networks in empirical studies (Latour, 1999b; Latour, 2005). Symmetry relates to the symmetrical treatment of humans/non-humans and is intended to 'flatten' hierarchies pertaining to what might be considered more important in a situation (Law, 2004b). For example, many social science theories consider human action as being more important than other material relations that occur in the workplace, which can lead to practices being overlooked (Latour, 2005). The concept of symmetry stems from how humans and non-humans are treated within the network, and has been the subject of controversy (Latour, 1999a), which is discussed later. The critiques of symmetry have prompted discussion and debate contributing to after-ANT. Finally, the concept of multiple worlds has developed through writers such as Law (1999) and Mol (1998, 2002, 2010) to describe the irreducibility of the dualism of single and multiple. Multiple worlds relate to difference; rather than triangulating using different perspectives to consolidate meaning into a singularity, ANT unfolds what might appear to be singularities to explore the complex and diverse worlds they inhabit. The 'after-ANT' turn is outlined by some of its leading authors in *Actor Network Theory and After* (Law and Hassard, 1999), describing how ANT has been presented and what it could become.

Attuning to networks

The networks to which Latour (2005) refers are conceptual and dynamic, rather than something 'out there'; they are about the translations and effects that occur when elements come together or 'assemble'. An assemblage can be described as a group of objects, people, ideas, and processes that have a relation to each other; what makes up the assemblage can be described as heterogeneous materials held together by forces and flows (Fenwick, Nerland and Jensen, 2011). Networks can be conceived of in practice as associations and relational forces, but these do not need to have the 'shape' of a typical network, such as a transport map or electrical system; these could just as easily be a piece of music or a workplace procedure (Latour, 2005). The network is of interest because of how it exposes relations and explores the stability, movement and strength of connections: networks can take account of what has been overlooked (Latour, 1999a) by focusing on the effects of relations rather than the entities themselves. The term 'network' and its prominence in ANT has become problematic for several different reasons. Latour (1999b) identifies how networks have become more closely associated with the internet. There is also the connotation that networks are socially constructed, and easily visualised with 'nodes' (people or objects) that are connected (usually in straight and even lines) to each other.

The term 'black-box' has been used in ANT to describe how processes become stable and immutable, and any internal complexity becomes taken for granted (Fenwick and Edwards, 2010). The idea of becoming taken for granted implies that some processes become hidden. Law (2004b) describes the method assemblage as an approach which implicates the ideas of presence: in other words, by making something present other things are being made absent. The idea of giving 'voice' to objects is a way of making objects visible and not overlooked (Latour, 2005). An object or representation renders something present, with absences being either manifest in what is present, or rendered 'other' through being repressed or hidden. The method assemblage is about resonance, amplifying some things and silencing others (Law, 2004b), and describes the way in which things become visible in networks. Another way in which networks present visibility is through what Latour (2004, 2005) refers to as 'matters of fact' and 'matters of concern'. Controversies are settled and presented as 'matters of fact', which are accepted as objective and naturalised. There is also a risk of collapsing everything into the network: where to 'cut the network' is a dilemma that the researcher is constantly required to justify (McLean and Hassard, 2004). One of the problems in cutting the network is knowing what to include and what to exclude. As mentioned earlier, the dilemma becomes one of favouring some actants over others. Early, or classic, ANT has been criticised for foregrounding the 'big' or most prominent actors in ANT accounts (McLean and Hassard, 2004), thereby relegating other actants to the background or context. This leads into discussions on the imbalance or asymmetry that can occur in ethnographic accounts, and explains how ANT has held on to the tenet of symmetry despite numerous criticisms. This is discussed in more detail later.

Translation

One of the most important features of networks is the way in which entities are transformed by other entities in the network. That is to say, when practice is enacted, the connections and associations that take place transform the entities enacting those connections. This is referred to as translation. Latour and Woolgar (2013) describe the process of translation as one in which activities are transformed through a network of inscription devices. Inscription devices are networks of elements that construct a reality (Law, 2004b). Latour and

Woolgar's (2013) ethnography of laboratories presented the term 'inscription device' to describe a system or process of translation that occurred in laboratory practices. An inscription device usually refers to a system that transforms materials and names the outputs, thereby making relations between instruments and traces; for example, the process of turning laboratory tests into scientific papers. In ANT, the focus of interest is what things *do* rather than what they *mean* (Fenwick, Nerland and Jensen, 2011), and *doing* brings about change. This is significant in education, as traditional models of learning are built on the assumption that learning and knowledge are stable, essentialised 'things' which can be 'transferred' and 'acquired' without change (Boud and Hager, 2012). ANT challenges these assumptions by focusing on the relations and associations that occur as entities interact; new connections not only create new networks, but the entities themselves are changed through translation. For example, Berg and Goorman (1999) argue about the contingency of medical information, as the information exists only in association with surrounding information. The process of translation can be described as traduction, or treason (trahison) (Brown, 2002). This allows networks to be conceptualised as dynamic and unstable, rather than causal or predictive. In practice, translation can occur through enactments and devices in the network.

Networks in education research

The concept of networks has been applied to prominent studies that have informed much empirical work in the field of ANT in education (Nespor, 2014; Sørensen, 2009). Nespor's work followed two disciplines (physics and management) in post-compulsory education. Nespor (2014) was keen to emphasise, following Latour (2005), that an ANT lens provides a way to describe and move data rather than to explain it. Nespor focuses on movement and space/time to describe learning and knowledge:

> [P]eople move through space materially, and simultaneously move and construct space-time through practices of representation, and what we call 'learning' are segments of motion which follow the shapes of more stable institutional or disciplinary networks.
>
> (Nespor, 2014, p. 131)

He explains that having knowledge means that you participate in an actor-network, which can be a field of practice; in other words, a 'discipline'. Participation involves movement around that field, around networks of power. Nespor continues:

> To understand learning and knowledge it's just as essential to trace out the network structures and the political economy that sustains them as it is to study students' experiences in specific settings of pedagogy or practice.
>
> (Nespor, 2014, p. 132)

So far it has been demonstrated that the concept of networks moves far beyond a semantic map of nodes and connections. As Nespor highlights in the above quote, networks are also about describing the 'political economy'. Another facet of networks is how power is enacted. Translations and relations constitute power through assemblages and networks. For example, Fenwick and Edwards (2010) describe the power in educational spaces such as a lecture theatre, where there is a screen and stage at the front with seats fixed in this direction. At the time of writing, during the 2020 COVID-19 pandemic, the significance of seating in relation to social distancing has suddenly been catapulted to the fore of how society is enacted. Actor-networks describe dynamic, shifting, mutating conceptions that help to trace power relations through a process of translations between entities (Fenwick and Edwards, 2010). What might be referred to as the properties (an essentialist term) of networks include descriptions of the ways in which actants engage with the network. Specifically, these need to be considered alongside the phenomenon of translation, and how this transforms actants as they assemble and form connections within a network. However, some actants become so well established and performed within a network that they can be transported without transformation: as Latour describes, like can-nonballs. Immutable mobiles are actants within a network that hold their shape of relations sufficiently to be able to be displaced without transforming (Latour, 1987). Some immutable mobiles can become Obligatory Passage Points (OPPs) (Callon, 1984). Latour (1993) describes OPPs as a point at which actants are obliged to pass to continue acting. Latour (1993) uses the example of the trans-mission of the gonorrhoea microbe from mother to baby: in this case, the OPP is the eyelashes of a new-born infant, to which the microbe adheres during the birthing process; without this attachment, it would be difficult for the microbe to spread. The OPP provides a way of describing the order of enactments, the path of actants, and where work needs to focus to continue the practice. OPPs can also be described as assemblages where relations within the network are required to pass, and can affect the flow of power in a network (Fenwick and Edwards, 2010).

ANT and symmetry

The concept of symmetry in ANT distinguishes it from other socio-material theories, such as CHAT and complexity theory. The ANT researcher is not seeking the depth and meaning through actions, but a focus on the actions themselves and what unfolds in a particular situation, without privileging humans. As Mulcahy (2014) suggests, sociocultural approaches consider mate-rials as being mediated by humans, with humans remaining at the centre; alter-natively, socio-material approaches seek to de-centre the human by focusing on relations and effects, rather than separate entities. What we see in everyday practice has inevitably come from agency sources that are spread throughout out time and space. As Latour (2005) describes:

any given interaction seems to overflow with elements which are already in the situation coming from some other time, some other place, and generated by some other agency.

(Latour, 2005, p. 166)

Whereas other social theories might trace agency, motivations, intentions, history, and underlying meaning, what is of interest to ANT is the actions and interactions between entities that grow in a flat, rhizomic way, without seeking deeper meaning and causes. Returning to the origin or source of agency is rejected in favour of the here and now (Latour, 2005). As an example, visualise entering a workplace such as a hospital or a bank or a manufacturing plant where you are confronted by practices that are an interaction of people and things; the agency of the action cannot be traced back to the source. A recent example might be drawn from the case of Dr Hadiza Bawa-Garba, whose recent suspension from the medical council was overturned in light of the circumstances within which she worked. As Latour (2005) puts it:

A plaintiff summoned to face the judge discovers the edifice of law firmly in place and the Old Bailey building as ancient as London. A worker, who labours all day on the floor of a sweatshop, discovers quite quickly that his fate has been settled by invisible agents who are hidden behind the office walls at the other end of the shop. A pedestrian with a sprained ankle learns in the doctor's office about her skeleton and the physiology that predate the time of her accident. A local 'informant', prodded by the questions of a visiting ethnographer, realizes that most of his habits of thought are coming from places and agencies over which he has no control.

(Latour, 2005, p. 166)

An ANT sensibility holds that practice can be better understood by focusing on relations between entities that form networks of practices. Rather than separate and categorise students, staff, patients, pens, paper, PCs, wards, beds, reports, tests, and so on, ANT focuses on the effects that are produced when these entities relate to each other and form networks. Central to this is the idea that entities do not have an essential, unchangeable presence, but that all things exist by their associations with other things. Unlike many social theories that strive to produce representations of the social by producing patterns and models, ANT is non-representational and descriptive. This enables the researcher to approach a situation and record actions, relations and practices with a view that all things acting are treated equally, or symmetrically.

As previously described, ANT focuses on networks and relations, at the dynamic and shifting associations between entities rather than fixed individual entities. This raises questions about how the researcher (a human) represents humans and non-humans, and about how non-humans participate in the social (McLean and Hassard, 2004). Law (1992, p. 383) describes how humans are positioned within symmetry: 'what counts as a person is an effect generated by a network of heterogeneous, interacting materials'. In relation to education, one could ask, what is a student? Or, more pertinently, how is a student performed into being? Clarke (2002) provides an empirical description of students as 'subjects and objects of knowledge [that] can be observed empirically as entities circulating in networks' (Clarke, 2002, p. 107). Clarke (2002, p. 120) concludes by stating:

> The contribution of actor-network theory to this task is to provide a rich fund of ready-made examples to learn from, and to suggest points of departure for new stories about how people learn what they learn, and how adult educators decide what other people ought to know.

This quote supports the notion of ANT as a sensibility that considers what things do rather than what they are; what effects elements have within their particular networks and what associations are formed. In terms of how knowledge is conceptualised:

> knowing, or coming to know something, is regarded as something that emerges as an effect of the socio-material arrangements that gather together and are performed into being through the continual transactions.
>
> (Ahn et al., 2015)

The idea of symmetry relates to how elements within a network are treated. In many social science approaches, humans are considered as the source of all agency. This has led to social science studies privileging the human. Symmetry describes how dualisms are challenged in ANT, for example, humans are not foregrounded in favour of non-humans, as commonly happens in sociological theory. In ANT, symmetry originates from the idea of modernism and the bifurcation of nature and science. Symmetry is also about approaching a situation without taking on the assumptions of whether something is scientifically true or false (Law, 2004b); by privileging truth over falsity, one enters the world asymmetrically, with a leaning towards some assumptions over others. ANT argues that assemblages are best described symmetrically; that is to say, not in terms of true and false beliefs shaped by history, but in terms of how a situation is shaped by the natural and social world Law (2004b). The risk of asymmetry is to ignore actants and relations that are significant but presumed unimportant. The ANT concept of symmetry holds that these assumptions and values have the potential to skew 'how we see the world'; indeed, the preceding statement is invalidated by symmetry, as 'we' are inseparable from the world, and our 'seeing' does not validate any foregrounding of important actors. Following this logic to its inevitable conclusion, symmetry, by not privileging the human, then gives voice to nonhumans. The choice of language here is significant: the selection of the word 'non-human' rather than 'object' is because the term 'object' immediately conjures a 'subject' (Sayes, 2014); the term 'things' has similar connotations and represents a body of thought about how nonhumans are already situated in a human world. Ascribing agency to nonhumans has implications as to how materials are politically involved and enmeshed in the social. Abrahamsson et al.'s (2015) description of how Omega 3 is ingested and becomes part of the human that ingests it goes beyond a passive description of the place of food in biological activity. Abrahamsson et al. (2015) conclude that it is relational materialism that acts, things do not act alone; it is not about 'what' acts, but how the actions push and pull. Rather than saying 'causing' and 'acting', we should be saying 'affording' and 'responding'; 'caring' and 'tinkering'.

In ANT, symmetry has become known as treating objects the same as humans, which has led to scepticism by a number of authors in the field. For example, some writers assert that ANT ascribes agency and intent to non-humans, to allow them to act and influence a situation in a particular way (McLean and Hassard, 2004; Pels, 1996). The awkwardness of dealing with symmetry has led to some ANT analyses either glossing over the subject or going too far and becoming radical. McLean and Hassard (2004) describe this dilemma as symmetrical absence or symmetrical absurdity. Symmetrical absence can lead to exclusion of the idea or a preference for asymmetry. These concerns have been taken up in post-humanist approaches which propose 'interviewing the object' as a way of giving voice to non-humans (Adams and Thompson, 2016) and authors such as Bruni (2005) have explored this in ANT accounts of clinical work practices. Some of the criticism aimed at ANT, and in particular, symmetry, are outlined and discussed in the next section.

ANT will eat itself: key critiques of symmetry

The idea of the socio-material is to include the material in sociological accounts, where traditionally the material would be overlooked because of the focus on human activity (Fenwick and Edwards, 2010). This shift in thinking brings with it controversy, particularly against the backdrop of humanism in sociocultural theories. Arguments against ANT challenge the relegated position of the human as the subject, and raise moral implications of flattening reality so that a door has as much significance as the person walking through it (for key critiques, see: Collins and Yearly, 1992; McLean and Hassard, 2004; Miettinen, 1999; Pels, 1996). The argument of Collins and Yearly (1992) in *Epistemological Chicken* is that ANT produces overly detailed accounts of practice that are dull and irrelevant. However, McLean and Hassard (2004) contend that detail is important, even though it is sometimes prosaic; we ignore the mundane to our peril, because this is where the work is situated. Collins and Yearly (1992) argue that ANT has not added anything significantly new to the field of the Sociology of Scientific Knowledge (SSK), and that the way ANT is presented tends to over-claim its relevance to sociology. Miettinen (1999) argues that ANT's main methodological flaws render ANT unsuitable for the study of innovation. These flaws are described as:

> the problem of structuring the analysis of the network and selecting the relevant elements or actor, the problem of silent actors, and the problem of human capability or intentionality in explaining the establishment of network associations.
>
> (Miettinen, 1999, p. 181)

Pels (1996) appeals for alternative positions of symmetry, rather than the radical stance taken by Latour and other ANT theorists. Pels' (1996) argument is that approaching a situation symmetrically creates distance and detachment that may be translated as disinterested, dehumanising, apolitical, and amoral. Other writers have argued about the unsuitability of ANT in particular situations. McLean and Hassard (2004) also call for caution in relation to symmetry, citing examples where symmetry had either been omitted or taken *ad absurdum*. However, some of ANT's greatest critiques come from the originators themselves (to name but a few: Brown and Capdevila, 1999; Latour, 1999b; Law and Hassard, 1999; Mol, 2010). Some of these critiques were included in a collection of papers that formed a seminal work on 'after-ANT' (Law and Hassard, 1999).

After-ANT: multiple worlds

The movement of after-ANT created space for other ideas of relational and material ways of considering situations. As Sørensen (2009) observed in her ethnography of education, the networks concept was helpful for empirical descriptions, but did not always 'fit' with her ethnography. Other concepts in ANT, particularly in after-ANT, draw from spatiality and fluidity, which Sørensen found to be more appropriate to attune to ambiguity in the data. ANT writers such as Mol (2010) and Law (2004b) began to develop a wider range of metaphors to describe the messiness of practice, and to enable descriptions to include difference, uncertainty, ambivalence, and ambiguity. There are subtle differences between these terms that need to be explained before they are applied empirically. Uncertainty signposts to doubt and a lack of conformity; there must also be an assumption of the norm and how things are categorised. Ambiguity refers to an openness, a resistance to consolidating or closure; a slipperiness of meaning. The term 'ambivalence' is different from uncertainty and ambiguity because it carries with it a certain energy. Ambivalence in human thought in the field of health behaviour change has been described as an 'accountant's balance sheet' (Mason and Butler, 2010). It pertains to a polarisation of thought and oscillation between these poles. Rather than 'sitting on the fence', ambivalence can point to dissonance and angst. Moving away from psychology and towards the socio-material, ambivalence implies force and agency in the relation between heterogeneous objects that fluctuates rather than being unidirectional, creating what Fenwick and Edwards (2010) refer to as 'strain'.

In an ANT analysis, difference is followed, troubled and unfolded in divergent trajectories, allowing detail to emerge. As the authors (Fenwick and Edwards, 2010) point out, many models and theories attempt to smooth out complexity, whereas ANT looks down into the baroque detail. Bleakley (2012) likens the divergency of ANT as the opposite of triangulation, throwing open possibilities rather than consolidating difference into a single point; and as Latour (2005) suggests, ANT is more like the oligopticon, seeing little but seeing well, as opposed to the panopticon, which sees all. This process of unfolding brings us back to the dilemma of where to 'cut the network'; like Zeno's paradox, the opening out becomes *regressus in infinitum*. This line of argument also draws attention to the idea of approaching something that appears as a singularity (e.g. a medical condition) but unfolds in practice into a multiplicity.

Multiplicity and ontological politics

Mol's (2002) ethnography of atherosclerosis and how this is enacted in hospital practice draws attention to the multiplicity of 'worlds', how these worlds 'hang together', and how enactments become political acts. The term 'praxiography' was described by Mol (2002) as an ethnographic approach that explores uncertainty and difference, maintaining the messiness of practice. As Law (2004b) describes it, praxiography allows for the exploration of how objects are continually enacted. Mol (2002) employed praxiography to explore the idea of what atherosclerosis 'is' and how this situated and enacted in practice. Through studying these enactments, Mol (2002) described how atherosclerosis, far from being a singularity, was actually performed as a multiple. However, this did not extend to being many different things: the condition is not plural. The multiple enactments signposted to different worlds of practice where atherosclerosis 'is' a tissue sample on a slide, and an account of symptoms by the patient, and a diagnosis by the doctor.

Continuing the notion that practice networks produce reality, Law (2004b) suggests that these different realities can be viewed as different worlds; realities are produced along the way, which Law (2009) refers to as 'collateral realities'. The conditions of possibility that exist within a world are shaped by intervention and performance (Mol, 1998). By focusing on the 'world' produced by practice, the researcher can appreciate the particular rather than the general, and can attune to the relations and practices within it and develop a sensibility within that world (Law, 2004b). This is a departure from the idea of the 'singular' reality 'out there' that is propagated by Euro-American metaphysics and dominates scientific thought.

Mol (2002) also builds on the idea of multiple worlds to conceptualise how the same worlds can exist side by side, and if they interact or subsume one another. In order to regulate difference, Mol summarises the different ways in which worlds exist to either reconcile difference or sustain multiplicity. Law (2004b) further develops this idea. Reconciliation of worlds is achieved in different ways: *layering*, of which the 'body multiple' is an example of an underlying condition bringing about symptoms and diagnoses which conflict; *a single narrative*, where the story of a phenomenon is smoothed over; *translations*, where one process turns into another or is converted; *submission*, where one world dominates another; and *rationalisation*, where inconsistences are glossed over by narrative. Alternatively, multiplicity can be sustained through mutual exclusion, creating different or composite objects, and location in different places. Multiplicity can be disguised, but by observing practice through praxiography, these multiplicities can become evident. The implication of considering multiple worlds is that it presents questions regarding how worlds are conceptualised and treated, rather than being obscured (Fenwick, Edwards and Sawchuk, 2011).

If one accepts the idea that practice precedes reality (rather than the Euro-American metaphysical standpoint that reality exists 'out there' and therefore precedes practice), then it follows that because there are multiple practices, there are therefore multiple realities (Mol, 2002). If there are multiple realities, then there must be ways of reconciling or sustaining this multiplicity. Following the idea that sometimes worlds submit to other worlds, there must be scenarios when one version of reality dominates another. The notion of ontological politics challenges the conditions of possibilities that exist in different worlds, as there are different (political) reasons for enacting one world over another. Bleakley (2012) describes ANT as a research practice that challenges conventional evidence in medical education by exploring multiple possibilities rather than a singular meaning. This emphasises the difference in conceptualising research methods, and how evidence-based practice in medical education has a fixed notion of rigour that can be challenged.

ANT in practice

The arguments for attending to the socio-material are compelling, especially for practitioners and researchers who work with equipment and technology in the workplace. It appears intuitive that materials are brought to bear in the workplace as these are visible and an intrinsic part of practice. The challenge, however, is in moving away from the idea that we need to compartmentalise and categorise in a conventional manner, ultimately for the purposes of reducing and generalising data. Many research approaches treat data in this way: the researcher gathers a large amount of information and it is then necessary to condense it. ANT, however, moves in the opposite direction. Ambivalences are troubled and unfolded, ambiguities are explored in a baroque 'ponds within ponds' way to draw out more, not less, detail (Law, 2004a). This poses a problem for researchers: how is the analysis representative of the whole, how can it be packaged and made sense of? The answer is not in representing but in describing detail. Analysis then comes out of the emerging detail, rather than in the reductionist and representational decisions of the researcher.

Attending to language

As discussed before, because ANT draws from post-structuralist traditions, the meaning of particular words is shaped by their association with other words (Law and Hassard, 1999; Mol, 2010). ANT subscribes to the view that meaning is contingent, therefore meaning will be translated rather than transported (Law, 2006). The word 'network' is an example of where the use of a word has changed with the introduction of the internet (Latour, 2005). The meanings of other words also carry connotations and connections with meaning that might not be intended. For example, (Nespor, 2014) and (Sørensen, 2009) write about the use of the word 'performance' and how this becomes associated, in the social sciences, with Goffman's theatre analogies; this meaning is incongruent with the use of performance in ANT, which uses the word to describe how situations unfold in space/time rather than describing what is 'backstage'. Mol (2002) advocates the use of the word 'enact'; although this has other associations, she explicitly asks her readers to approach the word as 'fresh' (Mol, 2002, 2010). The word 'activity' is sometimes used in empirical descriptions, which is associated with human action and therefore is asymmetrical (Sørensen, 2009). McLean and Hassard (2004) engage with controversies directed towards ANT and symmetry in terms of its distancing from the human (Pels, 1996), potential amorality (Miettinen, 1999), and for pushing epistemology beyond reasonable philosophical arguments. These arguments cause tensions to surface when attempting to de-centre the human, as ultimately it is a human employing the language to describe reality; this dilemma could almost be described as Munchausian, as to separate the human from language would be 'to pull oneself into existence out of the swamp of nothingness by one's own hair' (Nietzsche, 2003, p. 21). ANT descriptions require sensitive language towards materials and a balanced treatment of humans and non-humans. Authors have identified the different ways in which language is used to describe humans and non-humans as changing register (Hassard, Kelemen and Cox, 2012) or being out of tune (Sørensen, 2009), which indicates asymmetrical treatment. Regarding humans, ANT's position is that agency and intentionality does not reside with the individual human, but is instead an effect of associations within a network (Fenwick and Edwards, 2010).

To address these dilemmas, some authors have put forward terms that follow the ontological nuances of ANT. Fenwick (2014) uses the terms: attending, attuning, noticing, tinkering, and interrupting, to focus on workplace learning. Abrahamsson et al. (2015) articulate a preference for the words affording, responding, caring, and tinkering over the words causing and acting. In this book, the term 'attuning' is used to express resonance and fine-tuning, in favour of words that imply unidirectional movement or cause and effect. The term 'invite' is used in relation to materials and how they are situated in practice. It is an alternative expression to 'afford' which has connotations in cognitive psychology. In this book, the word 'invite' is preferred over 'afford', as the former is considered as performative: entities are actively invited into networks, rather than 'affordances' passively waiting to be taken up.

In the next chapter the three ANT dimensions (networks, symmetry, and multiple worlds) are brought to bear on an empirical research study conducted in a hospital setting.

References

Abrahamsson, S., Bertoni, F., Mol, A. and Martín, R.I. (2015). Living with omega-3: New materialism and enduring concerns. *Environment and Planning D: Society and Space*, 33(1), pp. 4–19.

Adams, C. and Thompson, T.L. (2016). *Researching a posthuman world: Interviews with digital objects*. London: Palgrave Macmillan.

Ahn, S., Rimpiläinen, S., Theodorsson, A., Fenwick, T. and Dahlgren, M.A. (2015). Learning in technology-enhanced medical simulation: Locations and knowings. *Professions and Professionalism*, 5(3).

Berg, M. and Goorman, E. (1999). The contextual nature of medical information. *International Journal of Medical Informatics*, 56(1), pp. 51–60.

Bleakley, A. (2012). The proof is in the pudding: Putting actor-network-theory to work in medical education. *Medical Teacher*, 34(6), pp. 462–467.

Bleakley, A., Bligh, J. and Browne, J. (2011). *Medical education for the future: Identity, power and location*. Heidelberg: Springer Science & Business Media.

Boud, D. and Hager, P. (2012). Re-thinking continuing professional development through changing metaphors and location in professional practices. *Studies in Continuing Education*, 34(1), pp. 17–30.

Brown, S.D. (2002). Michel Serres. *Theory, Culture & Society*, 19(3), pp. 1–27.

Brown, S.D. and Capdevila, R. (1999). Perpetuum mobile: Substance, force and the sociology of translation. *The Sociological Review*, 47 (suppl 1), pp. 26–50.

Bruni, A. (2005). Shadowing software and clinical records: On the ethnography of nonhumans and heterogeneous contexts. *Organization*, 12(3), pp. 357–378.

Callon, M. (1984). Some elements of a sociology of translation: Domestication of the scallops and the fishermen of St Brieuc Bay. *The Sociological Review*, 32 (suppl 1), pp. 196–233.

Clarke, J. (2002). A new kind of symmetry: Actor-network theories and the new literacy studies. *Studies in the Education of Adults*, 34(2), pp. 107–122.

Collins, H. and Yearly, S. (1992). Epistemological chicken. In: A. Pickering, ed., *Science as Practice and Culture*. Chicago, IL: The University of Chicago Press, pp. 301–326.

Czarniawska, B. and Hernes, T. eds. (2020). *Actor-network theory and organizing*. 2nd ed. Lund: Studentlitteratur.

Engeström, Y. (2001). Expansive learning at work: Toward an activity theoretical reconceptualization. *Journal of Education and Work*, 14(1), pp. 133–156.

Falk, A.L., Hopwood, N. and Dahlgren, M.A. (2017). Unfolding practices: A sociomaterial View of interprofessional collaboration in health care. *Professions and Professionalism*, 7(2).

Fenwick, T. (2014). Sociomateriality in medical practice and learning: Attuning to what matters. *Medical Education*, 48(1), pp. 44–52.

Fenwick, T. and Edwards, R. (2010). *Actor-network theory in education*. London: Routledge.

Fenwick, T., Edwards, R. and Sawchuk, P. (2011). *Emerging approaches to educational research: Tracing the socio-material*. Abingdon: Routledge.

Fenwick, T., Nerland, M. and Jensen, K. eds. (2014). *Professional Learning in Changing Contexts*. Oxon: Routledge.

Fleck, L. (1981). *Genesis and development of a scientific fact*. Chicago, IL: The University of Chicago Press.

Goldszmidt, M. and Faden, L. (2016). Is medical education ready to embrace the socio-material? *Medical Education*, 50(2), pp. 162–164.

Gorur, R. (2012). ANT on the PISA Trail: Following the statistical pursuit of certainty. In: T. Fenwick and R. Edwards, eds., *Researching education through actor-network theory*. Chichester: John Wiley & Sons, pp. 60–77.

Harman, G. (2010). *Prince of networks: Bruno Latour and metaphysics*. Melbourne: Re.press.

Hassard, J., Kelemen, M. and Cox, J.W. (2012). *Disorganization theory: Explorations in alternative organizational analysis*. London: Routledge.

Ibrahim, E.F., Richardson, M.D. and Nestel, D. (2015). Mental imagery and learning: A qualitative study in orthopaedic trauma surgery. *Medical Education*, 49(9), pp. 888–900.

Kanger, L. (2017). Mapping 'the ANT multiple': A comparative, critical and reflexive analysis. *Journal for the Theory of Social Behaviour*, early view online. DOI: 10.1111/jtsb.12147.

Latour, B. (1987). *Science in action: How to follow scientists and engineers through society*. Cambridge, MA: Harvard University Press.

Latour, B. (1993). *The pasteurization of France*. Cambridge, MA: Harvard University Press.

Latour, B. (1999a). On recalling ANT. In: J. Law and J. Hassard, eds., *Actor network theory and after*. Oxford: Blackwell Publishing, pp. 15–25.

Latour, B. (1999b). *Pandora's hope: Essays on the reality of science studies*. Cambridge, MA: Harvard University Press.

Latour, B. (2004). Why has critique run out of steam? From matters of fact to matters of concern. *Critical Inquiry*, 30(2), pp. 225–248.

Latour, B. (2005). *Reassembling the social: An introduction to actor-network-theory*. Oxford: Oxford University Press.

Latour, B. (2012). *We have never been modern*. Cambridge, MA: Harvard University Press.

Latour, B. and Woolgar, S. (2013). *Laboratory life: The construction of scientific facts*. Princeton, NJ: Princeton University Press.

Law, J. (1992). Notes on the theory of the actor-network: Ordering, strategy, and heterogeneity. *Systemic Practice and Action Research*, 5(4), pp. 379–393.

Law, J. (1999). After ANT: Complexity, naming and topology. In: J. Law and J. Hassard, eds., *Actor network theory and after*. Oxford: Blackwell Publishing, pp. 1–14.

Law, J. (2004a). And if the global were small and noncoherent? Method, complexity, and the baroque. *Environment and Planning D: Society and Space*, 22(1), pp. 13–26.

Law, J. (2004b). *After method: Mess in social science research*. London: Routledge.

Law, J. (2006). Traduction/trahison: Notes on ANT. *Convergencia, UAEM, Mexico* (42), pp. 32–57.

Law, J. (2009). *'Collateral realities', version of 29th December 2009*. Available at: http://www.heterogeneities.net/publications/Law2009CollateralRealities.pdf [Accessed 11 Nov. 2017].

Law, J. and Hassard, J. eds. (1999). *Actor network theory and after*. Oxford: Blackwell Publishing.

Law, J. and Singleton, V. (2000). *This is not an object*. Lancaster: Centre for Science Studies, Lancaster University. Available at: http://www.comp.lancs.ac.uk/sociology/papers/Law-Singleton-This-is-Not-an-Object.pdf. Last accessed on 15th November 2017.

Mason, P. and Butler, C.C. (2010). *Health behavior change E-book*. Edinburgh: Elsevier Health Sciences.

McMurtry, A., Rohse, S. and Kilgour, K.N. (2016). Socio-material perspectives on inter-professional team and collaborative learning. *Medical Education*, 50(2), pp. 169–180.

McLean, C. and Hassard, J. (2004). Symmetrical absence/symmetrical absurdity: Critical notes on the production of actor-network accounts. *Journal of Management Studies*, 41(3), pp. 493–519.

Michael, M. (1996). *Constructing identities: The social, the nonhuman and change*. London: Sage.

Miettinen, R. (1999). The riddle of things: Activity theory and actor-network theory as approaches to studying innovations. *Mind, Culture, and Activity*, 6(3), pp. 170–195.

Mol, A. (1998). Ontological politics. A word and some questions. *The Sociological Review*, 46, pp. 74–89.

Mol, A. (2002). *The body multiple: Ontology in medical practice*. Durham: Duke University Press.

Mol, A. (2010). Actor-network theory: Sensitive terms and enduring tensions. *Kölner Zeitschrift Für Soziologie Und Sozialpsychologie.Sonderheft*, 50, pp. 253–269.

Mulcahy, D. (2014). Re-thinking teacher professional learning: More than a representational account. In: T. Fenwick and M. Nerland, eds., *Reconceptualising professional learning: Socio-material knowledges, practices and responsibilities*. Abingdon: Routledge, pp. 52–66.

Nespor, J. (2014). *Knowledge in motion: Space, time and curriculum in undergraduate physics and management*. Abingdon: Routledge.

Nietzsche, F. (2003). *Beyond good and evil*. London: Penguin.

Pels, D. (1996). The politics of symmetry. *Social Studies of Science*, 26(2), pp. 277–304.

Sayes, E. (2014). Actor – Network Theory and methodology: Just what does it mean to say that nonhumans have agency? *Social Studies of Science*, 44(1), pp. 134–149.

Sørensen, E. (2009). *The materiality of learning: Technology and knowledge in educational practice*. Cambridge: Cambridge University Press.

Verran, H. (2001). *Science and an African logic*. Chicago, IL: University of Chicago Press.

Zukas, M. and Kilminster, S. (2014). The doctor and the blue form: Learning professional responsibility. In: T. Fenwick and M. Nerland, eds., *Reconceptualising professional learning: Sociomaterial knowledges, practices and responsibilities*. Abingdon: Routledge, pp. 38–51.

Chapter 3

The research setting

This chapter begins to weave together the empirical study and socio-material theory in the context of professional and practice learning. The study investigated SLISPs in a hospital setting. The historical and theoretical aspects of professional and workplace learning are described in this chapter, as part of the background to formal training for pre-service doctors and pharmacists. This chapter describes the setting and orientation of this research within quality improvement in healthcare and professional education. The chapter goes on to describe how this is situated in medical and pharmacy training. The current situation with the COVID-19 pandemic is then introduced as a possible research area for socio-material practice learning, such as ANT.

The research described in this book explores the detailed practices of SLISPs with the purpose of understanding how learning emerges as students carry out these projects. In order to describe how these practices have come about, it is necessary to explain some of the historical and political aspects of improvement science. The chapter begins by introducing improvement science as a systematic approach to quality improvement, and describes how the approach has been introduced to healthcare against a backdrop of service integration, public accountability, and a reliance on evidence-based practice. Improvement science is introduced in this chapter in terms of quality improvement methodologies in healthcare, and then described alongside other approaches. The argument progresses by describing how improvement science has had an impact on the requirement for healthcare staff to work inter-professionally and collectively, and the development of a curriculum that promotes these ways of working. The chapter goes on to situate the research in professional and practice learning by describing the historical trajectories in these fields. The chapter then brings together professional and practice education with SLISPs in the context of medical education to draw attention to the tensions between individualised and collective approaches to learning.

Improvement science: from Gold Standard to Silver Bullet

In healthcare, quality is defined as safe, effective, person-centred, timely, efficient, and equitable. Quality improvement, as defined by the Health Foundation, is:

> a systematic approach that uses a defined method to improve quality, with regard to better patient experience and outcomes achieved through changing the behaviour and organisation of healthcare providers.
>
> (Gabbay et al., 2014, p. 2)

Improvement science, in relation to the above definition, refers to a 'systematic approach' and 'defined method' to improvement that provides credence and validity to an improvement. Improvement in healthcare relates to patient safety, in that the patient experience is widely considered to be the most important aspect (Dahlgren, Dahlgren and Dahlberg, 2012). However, patient safety is related to many different factors, such as medical error, communication, and collaboration (Bleakley, 2014); other arguments, such as economic and organisational improvement, are also important contributors to patient safety. In this study, there is an emphasis on the approaches, methods, and tools promoted by the Institute for Healthcare Improvement's Open School Practicum (The Institute for Healthcare Improvement, 2017). The term 'improvement science' is not always used explicitly in the healthcare quality improvement literature, and other terms such as the Model for Improvement, which includes the PDSA (plan, do study, act) cycle, are referred to when discussing improvement (Langley et al., 2009).

Improvement science has been described as a gap between research (what is possible) and audit (what is actual) (The Evidence Centre, 2011), where research is exploratory and introduces new interventions, and audit is described as measuring against a standard (Lindsay, 2007). Improvement science has been adopted in the NHS as a way of coordinating quality improvement and the implementation of improvements in a more structured way. There are two central ideas to improvement science: (i) that an improvement is implemented and tested over time, and (ii) that improvements are identified by experts in the field (Rowe and Chapman, 2015). The Health Foundation defines improvement science as:

> *the application of a range of basic and applied sciences, delivered through a partnership of researchers and those who work in and use health services, with the aim of creating new knowledge and promoting strategies for the implementation of evidence-based healthcare, leading to improved processes and improved health outcomes for patients and populations.*
>
> (Lucas and Nacer, 2015, p. 2)

The above quote illustrates the expectation that interventions are informed by evidence, aligned with the values of evidence-based practice (EBP). Improvement science has also been described as the exchange and synthesis of knowledge to improve services (Bhattacharyya, Reeves and Zwarenstein, 2009), and 'a body of knowledge that describes how to improve safely and consistently' (The Evidence Centre, 2011, p. 6). Increasingly, discourses of 'what works', which describe how existing evidence is used in public services including quality improvement measures such as improvement science, are being proliferated in the health service as a response to the protracted time that is taken to put evidence into action and the paucity of available research needed to make decisions (Rowe and Chapman, 2015).

As discussed previously, there are different perspectives regarding what constitutes an improvement. For example, improvement for clinicians is more likely to be based on health outcomes; for patients, the effectiveness and delivery of services is most important; and for managers, the costs and benefits must also be considered (Gillam and Siriwardena, 2014). This means that there is no standard set of criteria for 'improvement', but there are elements that are desirable to achieve, such as quality, efficiency, equity, and value (Rowe and Chapman, 2015). In terms of patient care, systems and procedures can be complex, and this can affect what might constitute an improvement. In healthcare practices, patients often present with more than one condition, and require treatment on more than one ward with different specialists and medications. This affects the paperwork practices, patient records, and the movement of information within and outside wards. In terms of quality improvement, with numerous and overlapping practices being carried out simultaneously, what might be considered an improvement in one area might be contested in another. There is also the issue of consistency in practice to prevent errors and allow for professional judgement, rather than relying on a rigid protocol.

Improvements can address medical errors and streamline systems. There is a growing body of literature in the field of healthcare systems with the introduction of electronic and technological advances (Berg and Goorman, 1999; Cresswell, Worth and Sheikh, 2010). There are studies that describe how changes to paperwork procedures affect work on the wards, such as Allen's (2013) description of the Integrated Care Pathway, which was introduced to the ward as a single form that incorporated many other forms. The main finding of the research was that some staff found the form very helpful, but others found the form restrictive and preferred the original, multiple forms. Berg and Goorman (1999) also warned about the dangers of abstracting information that is contingent on practice, and the risks of information being misinterpreted and out of context. These examples illustrate the impact of mundane practices, and the necessity to explore processes in detail, particularly when considering an improvement or change. The examples also illustrate the potential instability created by an innovation, such as improvement science, balanced against the need for consistency in practice (Fenwick and Nerland, 2014). It is within this delicate balance that improvement science and SLISPs are conducted.

Student-led improvement science projects

The term 'SLISPs' has been created for this study rather than being an official or adopted term from the host university. This term refers to two important factors: (i) that the projects are led by students who are considered 'change agents' for improvement; and (ii) that the project follows improvement science methods. The host university terms the projects 'Student Selected Components' (SSC), which are identified in the medical curriculum as short projects which the students elect to take; however, this term also refers to other projects, such as work shadowing. SLISPs are guided by the IHI Open School templates and completed projects are posted onto the IHI site (The Institute for Healthcare Improvement, 2017). Some projects are also submitted to BMJ Quality Improvement Reports (Okwemba and Copeland, 2014). In some universities, improvement science has been introduced to the curriculum either as a mandatory or selected component (University of Stirling, Department of Health Sciences, 2015), as the focus of short, student-led projects. In pharmacology, students have been encouraged to participate as 'partners' in the development of the pharmacy curriculum. In a pharmacy study, this led to the improvement of the curriculum, where students highlighted that there was too much emphasis on clinical realism in scenario-based learning, and a lack of other situational factors, such as commercial pressures (Buchan et al., 2014).

The introduction of improvement science to learning programmes requires students to learn a set of strategies and approaches that may differ from those required for the rest of their course, relating to the identification, implementation, and management of improvements in the workplace, and then leading and working in clinical teams (The Institute for Healthcare Improvement, 2017). Although there is evidence to support the positive effects of students leading projects (Paterson et al., 2011) and of students leading quality improvement projects (Wong et al., 2010), the new configuration of their professional roles has sometimes been accompanied by negative consequences. Studies of quality improvement projects in the nursing curriculum have highlighted the discomfort and panic experienced by nursing students undertaking quality improvement projects (James et al., 2016). In terms of professional learning, the emphasis on audit and performance management might lead to deskilling, as professional judgement and expertise are less called upon. Working collaboratively in interdisciplinary teams presents new opportunities for defining professional practice, but there is also a need for translation as different worlds of practice combine. The instability that is required for innovation and change also interferes with the stability that is needed for continuity (Fenwick and Nerland, 2014). Therefore, there are questions that need to be raised. For example, are the practices of improvement science being critically examined in enough detail to challenge underlying assumptions and attend to tensions between collaborative learning and the scientific approach to improvement? How is learning configured when carrying out SLISPs and are there more appropriate ways in which we could conceptualise learning improvement science for medical students?

This study is situated at the intersection of different fields of education research. The SLISPs studied in this research were being undertaken as an elective part of the formal curriculum in medicine and pharmacy, situating the research in post-compulsory, formal education. The SLISPs were carried out in the workplace and, towards the end of the students' courses, bringing in aspects of workplace learning, practice, and professional learning. This brings different notions of learning into play. The 'student as change agent' and 'student-led' aspects of the SLISP projects draw from leadership, learning, and change, and from the concept of the leader as a subject expert (Rowe and Chapman, 2015). In the next section, several trajectories of learning are explored which intersect at the nexus where this study is situated. The section starts with professional learning, and tracks the history of approaches in this field. The next part discusses the practice turn, and how this has influenced professional learning through the exploration of practice. Finally, the section outlines medical education and how this enacts different types of learning through the practices of improvement science. This offers a rationale for the chosen approach of conceptualising learning as situated, contingent, and dynamic.

Practice and professional learning

Professional learning, as a field of inquiry, has undergone a number of changes in recent years, as scholarly practices become increasingly intertwined with the social (Hager, Lee and Reich, 2012). Learning is understood in organisation studies and education research as a socially situated activity (Gherardi, Nicolini and Odella, 1998). It has changed from having a focus on individuals and predictable input-output models to becoming systems-based with an emphasis on the sociocultural and socio-material. Traditionally, professional learning has favoured individualised approaches, such as training, workplace competencies, and individual learning plans (Fenwick, 2009). More recent sociocultural and socio-material approaches reconceptualise learning by moving away from the idea of learning as linear, individual, and transferrable and towards being dispersed, situated, and emergent. Hager, Lee and Reich (2012) propose five principles for theorising professional practice: knowing in practice; socio-material; embodied and relational; unstable, heterogeneous, and historical; and emergent. These are situated in two meta-traditions of neo-Aristotelian phronesis (relating to practical knowledge and ethics, action and experience as an alternative to the scientific-technical rationalities of traditional approaches) and post-Cartesian (challenging dualisms such as individual/social). These traditions and principles illustrate how practice, learning, and change have become reconceptualised. It is now widely acknowledged in the field that there are advantages to viewing professional learning as a phenomenon that emerges from relational effects between actants rather than something that happens to individual workers. Mulcahy (2014) describes the development of theorising professional practice in 'three tales of learning'. Tale One refers to learning as individual, cognitive, and acquisitional. In this 'tale', personal skills, knowledge, and attributes are valued. The second tale moves towards sociocultural approaches, conceptualising learning as participatory, practice-based, situated, embodied, and materially mediated. This allows learning to become viewed as social, moving away from skills and competencies and towards interdisciplinary and collaborative ways of learning. Finally, Tale Three conceptualises learning as socio-material. Unlike Tale Two, where materials are considered to be passive, Tale Three conceptualises learning as assemblage, where human and non-human are capable of acting.

Tale One has had an enduring influence in medical education and education in general. The study of medicine is rooted in a strong tradition of individual accountability, professionalism, and scientific method (Bleakley, 2012). The values of medical education foster approaches to education that support a high level of competence, autonomy, and authority (McKimm, Forrest and Thistlethwaite, 2017). The Flexner Report of 1910 had an overwhelming influence on medical education worldwide and the values upon which this was built still reverberate in medical education today (Bleakley, Bligh and Browne, 2011). The Flexner Report promoted the character of the 'good doctor' (Kuper, Whitehead and Hodges, 2013), promoting the idea of the heroic individual (Bleakley, 2014). The idea of learning as a cognitive process is reinforced in medical education by the assumption that doctors need to learn to be prepared for practice, rather than considering practice as part of learning (Dahlgren, Dahlgren and Dahlberg, 2012; Zukas and Kilminster, 2012). The metaphors of 'acquisition' and 'transfer' that are dominant in individualised learning approaches have been problematised in practice and professional learning; these metaphors can be limiting and imply that learning and knowledge are 'things' that can be moved without being changed (Boud and Hager, 2012).

In Tale Two, the notions of practice and participation have helped to shape the field of professional learning. This originates from the 'practice turn' where learning is now considered as embodied and material (Fenwick, Nerland and Jensen, 2014), socially ordered (Landri, 2012), and relational (Price et al., 2012). The idea of communities of practice, legitimate peripheral participation, and situated learning, have established a lexicon that allows learning to be conceptualised as collective rather than individual (Brown and Duguid, 1991; Lave and Wenger, 1991). The practice turn challenged how learning was conceptualised, rejecting Cartesian dualisms such as mind/body, subject/object, nature/science, turning instead to learning as enmeshed, situated, and ecological. For example, reflective practice is prominent in healthcare; however, this implies that 'thinking' is separate from 'doing', reinforcing the dualism (Fenwick, Nerland and Jensen, 2014). In approaching learning in this way, it is no longer possible to separate the knowing from the known, practice from learning, thinking from doing. This raises questions of how to articulate learning. The idea of communities of practice (CoPs) reconfigured learning in the workplace, but was critiqued for its limitations in terms of describing power relations and innovations (Fenwick, Nerland and Jensen, 2014; Fox, 2000; Roberts, 2006). Contu and Willmott (2003) claimed CoPs were aligned with managerial values and were embedded in relations of power. The concept of practice has been further theorised to gain a deeper understanding of professional learning; such as emphasising 'practice' in communities of practice (Contu and Willmott, 2003) and by referring to practices of community (Gherardi, 2012). The terms 'practice' and 'participation' start to decentre the individual in the articulation of learning and move towards distribution in the collective. Unfolding practice sensitivity as an 'embodied and materially mediated practice' (Landri, 2012) also introduces the concept of materiality.

Tale Three engenders the material turn, where socio-material approaches acknowledge practice and participation in learning as: (i) part of the whole system; (ii) interactions and relations between humans and non-humans; and (iii) learning and knowledge is embedded in action rather than internalised in a human participant (Fenwick, Edwards and Sawchuk, 2011). Learning and knowledge now become organising practices in human and non-human assemblages, rather than separate entities that can be possessed and measured. Reconceptualising learning as socio-material requires a shift in language and thinking. A number of theories have been introduced to facilitate the description of learning as socio-material. These include CHAT, complexity theory, new materialisms and ANT (Fenwick, Edwards and Sawchuk, 2011). Although CHAT is often included under the umbrella of socio-material theory, materials are considered to be mediated by humans (Fenwick, 2014), which would situate CHAT in Tale Two rather than Tale Three. In terms of improvement science, the document *Habits of an Improver* draws from psychologised models of learning to develop individual knowledge, skills, and habits (Lucas and Nacer, 2015). However, another guidance document, *Skilled for improvement*, espouses the values of community and collective learning (Gabbay et al., 2014), which is more aligned with Tale Two. This thesis draws from ANT, which situates the approach in Tale Three. ANT provides a radical approach to the socio-material, which focuses on the relational, spatial, and dynamic nature of learning and knowledge. The empirical research in this book explores SLISPs as a situated, practice-based, entwined experience, from which learning emerges through network effects rather than being a social or cognitive phenomenon (Ahn et al., 2015). By examining SLISPs with an ANT sensibility, we can begin to appreciate some of the detail and practice in its undertaking. Improvement science becomes a way of 'doing' improvement, a way of enacting interdisciplinary working.

Improvement science and medical education

The range of literature informing the research is drawn from different disciplines and traditions. The two main fields are quality improvement in healthcare and medical education. However, these fields also draw from other areas, such as healthcare processes and systems, quality improvement from other disciplines, education, and professional and practice learning. The studies of particular interest to this research also draw from socio-technical, socio-material, and ANT as theory and methodology. As part of the research project, I regularly attended reading groups and committees for implementation science where we discussed a number of current studies relating to implementation and improvement science. Although implementation science is different to improvement science, as the emphasis is on implementing change in a systematic way, there is much overlap with improvement science. These groups were pivotal for identifying key literature in the field. This included current studies in improvement science, healthcare, and education (Armstrong, Lauder and Shepherd, 2015; Davey et al., 2013; James et al., 2016; Lucas and Nacer, 2015; Paterson et al., 2011). Included in this were two recent studies, which described the educative experiences of nursing students as they undertook quality improvement projects (Armstrong, Lauder and Shepherd, 2015; James et al., 2016). The research also drew from quality improvement studies that did not have an education focus but contributed to the knowledge base of improvement science and quality improvement in healthcare (Aherne and Whelton, 2010; Bate et al., 2014; Buchan et al., 2014; Holden et al., 2013; Peden and Rooney, 2009; Rowe and Chapman, 2015). Of particular interest were education studies which drew from socio-material and ANT approaches in healthcare (Ahn et al., 2015; Bleakley, Bligh and Browne, 2011; Dahlgren, Dahlgren and Dahlberg, 2012; Falk, Hopwood and Dahlgren, 2017; Fenwick, 2014; Ibrahim, Richardson and Nestel, 2015; Zukas and Kilminster, 2014). Some of the ANT studies that were either situated in healthcare or education were very closely aligned with this research (Allen, 2013; Decuypere and Simons, 2016; Gorur, 2012; Law and Singleton, 2003; McMurtry, Rohse and Kilgour, 2016; Mol, 2002; Mulcahy, 2014; Nespor, 2012, 2014; Sørensen, 2009; Verran, 2001). Many ANT studies that influenced this research were seminal studies, but not situated in either education or healthcare (Latour, 1987; Latour and Porter, 1996; Latour and Woolgar, 2013; Latour, 1999; Star, 1990). There is also an emerging field in medical informatics and systems which draws from sociotechnical, socio-material and, specifically, ANT approaches (Allen, 2013; Berg and Goorman, 1999; Bruni, 2005; Cresswell, Worth and Sheikh, 2010). Thus, the literature informing this research was situated in many different and diverse fields and disciplines, which I drew together.

Learning in medical education and pharmacy studies

In the UK, the disciplines of medicine and pharmacy have been historically separated, leading to detached streams of education. This separation, and the recent measures taken to develop the relationship between medicine and pharmacy, are demonstrated in a statement released in 2011 by the ABPI (Association of the British Pharmaceutical Industry) in response to a report published by the RCP (Royal College of Physicians). The statement outlines changes to the ABPI Code of Practice, signalling a move towards more transparency, collaboration, and joint working. Doctors are trained in the field of medical education and their profession is governed by the GMC (General Medical Council). The GMC has published standards for undergraduate medical education, in the document *Tomorrow's Doctors* (General Medical Council Education Committee, 1993). The professional training of pharmacists is governed by the GPhC (General Pharmaceutical Council). In the UK, there are a growing number of academic courses for quality improvement in healthcare (Lucas and Nacer, 2015). In Scotland, medicine and pharmacy students are being encouraged to undertake projects that engage with quality improvement practices and inter-disciplinary working. The standards in Tomorrow's Doctors include working and learning in a multi-professional team to improve patient care professionalism; the standards of professionalism also comprises clinical, ethical, legal and moral responsibilities alongside respect, politeness, consideration, and trustworthiness (General Medical Council Education Committee, 1993). In addition to these standards, the document, *Habits of an Improver* (Lucas and Nacer, 2015), outlines the knowledge, skills, and habits required for undertaking quality improvement work. The research described in this book considers different types of improvement projects, including a longer quality improvement project for a Degree of Bachelor of Medical Science (BMSc) using improvement science methods, and an IHI (Institute for Healthcare Improvement) Practicum group project that comprised an SSC (for the medical student) and improvement projects for degree dissertations (for the pharmacy students). The IHI Open School Quality Improvement Practicum is a way of completing projects, with access to appropriate resources. The IHI provide guidelines for improvement projects and a facility for publishing projects online.

The curriculum developments described highlight a growing emphasis on inter-professional practice (Fenwick, 2014), inter-professional collaboration (Falk, Hopwood and Dahlgren, 2017), and inter-professional learning (Paterson et al., 2011) in healthcare education. With the increasing influence of patient safety, inter-professional working is becoming more prominent, and different approaches to learning have been developed to promote this (Ahn et al., 2015; Bleakley, 2014; Falk, Hopwood and Dahlgren, 2017). Simulation is one method whereby health professionals can work as a clinical team in a low-risk environment (Bleakley, 2014). In some cases, simulation is provided as an alternative to work-based learning. For example, pharmacy students cannot always get access to clinical placements, and simulation has been presented as an alternative (Buchan et al., 2014). Medical educators stress the importance of experienced-based learning (Dornan, Scherpbier and Boshuizen, 2009), problem-based learning (Dahlgren, Dahlgren and Dahlberg, 2012; Grant, Kinnersley and Field, 2012), and working in clinical environments (Paterson et al., 2011). Studies in inter-professional learning have explored how knowledge is shared between healthcare workers, and how collaboration practices unfold (Falk, Hopwood and Dahlgren, 2017; Fenwick, 2014). Socio-material approaches have been used to explore knowledge and learning in interdisciplinary working practices in medical education as a way of moving away from the dominant language of individualism (Bleakley, Bligh and Browne, 2011; McMurtry, Rohse and Kilgour, 2016) and cognitive approaches (Dahlgren, Dahlgren and Dahlberg, 2012).

Following on from the studies mentioned, this research provides an interruption to the literature on improvement science by applying the socio-material approach of ANT (Mitchell, 2020). The importance of this interruption has been demonstrated in a recent narrative review of the World Health Organisation Surgical Safety Checklist literature (Mitchell et al., 2017). The review argues that, since 2008, the literature on the checklist has been mainly focused on pre- and post-quantitative replication studies. The result of this is that the body of knowledge produced by the literature has not mobilised to produce a case either for or against the use of the checklist. As mentioned earlier in this chapter, the review calls for more detailed, qualitative studies to explore the sociocultural aspects of the checklist. In the same way, this research contributes to and complements the literature around improvement science, leading to a more comprehensive understanding of improvement science in practice. The purpose of this research is not to investigate the effectiveness of improvement science or the changes it brings about to organisations. Rather, this research looks at what learning SLISPs for health professionals, specifically medical students, means in practice. This will be useful for educators and policy makers to gain a more in-depth understanding of how improvement science is enacted, and to inform policy and curriculum decisions.

This chapter has outlined the development of improvement science in healthcare, and how this has been translated into medical education. Professional and practice learning were drawn from to trace the trajectories into socio-material and the new insights this can bring to medical education and education in general. In particular, the literature highlights interprofessional learning in healthcare and the increasing need to focus on collectives rather than individuals. The contribution of the study described in this book is at the nexus of improvement science medical education.

Medical education and COVID-19

As mentioned in this chapter, medical and pharmacy education promote interprofessional working practices through project working and simulation exercises. The current situation with COVID-19 necessitates the need for close professional working and organised procedures on hospital wards. In the UK, medical students and nursing staff in training have become enlisted in the workforce at an earlier stage than anticipated to cope with increased demands on healthcare during these times. It is hoped that the collaborative practices already in place have facilitated this development, and provide an organised and efficient response. Although it will be a while before we can attribute and trace the effects of education during the pandemic, hopefully SLISPs and applications of improvement science have provided an appropriate grounding for clinical staff to organise new procedures to deal with this challenging situation. The position of ANT-led research would be to enable staff to attune to new situations, and to notice relations between people and objects.

References

Aherne, J. and Whelton, J. eds. (2010). *Applying lean in healthcare: A collection of international case studies*. Boca Raton, FL: CRC Press.

Ahn, S., Rimpiläinen, S., Theodorsson, A., Fenwick, T. and Dahlgren, M.A. (2015). Learning in technology-enhanced medical simulation: Locations and knowings. *Professions and Professionalism*, 5(3).

Allen, D. (2013). Understanding context for quality improvement: Artefacts, affordances and socio-material infrastructure. *Health*, 17(5), pp. 460–477.

Armstrong, L., Lauder, W. and Shepherd, A. (2015). An evaluation of methods used to teach quality improvement to undergraduate healthcare students to inform curriculum development within preregistration nurse education: A protocol for systematic review and narrative synthesis. *Systematic Reviews*, 4(1), p. 8.

Bate, P., Robert, G., Fulop, N., Øvertveit, J. and Dixon-Woods, M. (2014). *Perspectives on context: A selection of essays considering the role of context in successful quality improvement*. London: Health Foundation.

Berg, M. and Goorman, E. (1999). The contextual nature of medical information. *International Journal of Medical Informatics*, 56(1), pp. 51–60.

Bhattacharyya, O., Reeves, S. and Zwarenstein, M. (2009). What is implementation research? Rationale, concepts, and practices. *Research on Social Work Practice*, 19(5), pp. 491–502.

Bleakley, A. (2012). The proof is in the pudding: Putting actor-network-theory to work in medical education. *Medical Teacher*, 34(6), pp. 462–467.

Bleakley, A., (2014). *Patient-centred medicine in transition: The heart of the matter*. Vol. 3. Heidelberg: Springer Science & Business Media.

Bleakley, A., Bligh, J. and Browne, J. (2011). *Medical education for the future: Identity, power and location*. Heidelberg: Springer Science & Business Media.

Boud, D. and Hager, P. (2012). Re-thinking continuing professional development through changing metaphors and location in professional practices. *Studies in Continuing Education*, 34(1), pp. 17–30.

Brown, J.S. and Duguid, P. (1991). Organizational learning and communities-of-practice: Toward a unified view of working, learning, and innovation. *Organization Science*, 2(1), pp. 40–57.

Bruni, A. (2005). Shadowing software and clinical records: On the ethnography of non-humans and heterogeneous contexts. *Organization*, 12(3), pp. 357–378.

Buchan, S., Regan, K., Filion-Murphy, C., Little, K., Strath, A., Rowe, I. and Vosper, H. (2014). Students as partners in a quality improvement approach to learning enhancement: A case study from a pharmacy undergraduate course. *Communicare*, 1(1).

Contu, A. and Willmott, H. (2003). Re-embedding situatedness: The importance of power relations in learning theory. *Organization Science*, 14(3), pp. 283–296.

Cresswell, K.M., Worth, A. and Sheikh, A. (2010). Actor-network theory and its role in understanding the implementation of information technology developments in healthcare. *BMC Medical Informatics and Decision Making*, 10(67).

Dahlgren, M.A., Dahlgren, L.O. and Dahlberg, J. (2012). Learning professional practice through education. In: P. Hager, A. Lee and A. Reich, eds., *Practice, learning and change: Practice-theory perspectives on professional learning*. Dordrecht: Springer, pp. 183–197.

Davey, P., Tully, V., Grant, A., Day, R., Ker, J., Marr, C., Mires, G. and Nathwani, D. (2013). Learning from errors: What is the return on investment from training medical students in incident review? *Clinical Risk*, 19(1), pp. 1–5.

Decuypere, M. and Simons, M. (2016). Relational thinking in education: Topology, sociomaterial studies, and figures. *Pedagogy, Culture & Society*, 24(3), pp. 371–386.

Dornan, T., Scherpbier, A. and Boshuizen, H. (2009). Supporting medical students' workplace learning: Experience-based learning (ExBL). *The Clinical Teacher*, 6(3), pp. 167–171.

The Evidence Centre. (2011). *Evidence scan: Improvement science*. London: The Health Foundation. Available at: www.health.org.uk/sites/health/files/Improvement Science.pdf [Accessed 11 Nov. 2017].

Falk, A.L., Hopwood, N. and Dahlgren, M.A. (2017). Unfolding practices: A sociomaterial View of interprofessional collaboration in health care. *Professions and Professionalism*, 7(2).

Fenwick, T. (2009). Making to measure? Reconsidering assessment in professional continuing education. *Studies in Continuing Education*, 31(3), pp. 229–244.

Fenwick, T. (2014). Knowledge circulations in inter-para/professional practice: A sociomaterial enquiry. *Journal of Vocational Education & Training*, 66(3), pp. 264–280.

Fenwick, T., Edwards, R. and Sawchuk, P. (2011). *Emerging approaches to educational research: Tracing the socio-material*. Abingdon: Routledge.

Fenwick, T. and Nerland, M. (2014). *Reconceptualising professional learning: Sociomaterial knowledges, practices and responsibilities*. Abingdon: Routledge.

Fenwick, T., Nerland, M. and Jensen, K. eds. (2014). *Professional learning in changing contexts*. Oxon: Routledge.

Fox, S. (2000). Communities of practice, Foucault and actor-network theory. *Journal of Management Studies*, 37(6), pp. 853–868.

Gabbay, J., le May, A., Connell, C. and Klein, J.H. (2014). *Skilled for improvement? The improvement skills pyramid*. London: The Health Foundation. Available at: www.health.org.uk/sites/health/files/SkilledForImprovement_pyramidtemplate.pdf [Accessed 11 Nov. 2017].

General Medical Council Education Committee. (1993). *Tomorrow's doctors: Recommendations on undergraduate medical education*. London: General Medical Council.

Gherardi, S. (2012). Why do practices change and why do they persist? Models of explanations. In: P. Hager, A. Lee and A. Reich, eds., *Practice, learning and change: Practice-theory perspectives on professional learning*. Dordrecht: Springer, pp. 217–231.

Gherardi, S., Nicolini, D. and Odella, F. (1998). Toward a social understanding of how people learn in organizations: The notion of situated curriculum. *Management Learning*, 29(3), pp. 273–297.

Gillam, S. and Siriwardena, A.N. (2014). *Quality improvement in primary care: The essential guide*. London: Radcliffe Publishing Ltd.

Gorur, R. (2012). ANT on the PISA trail: Following the statistical pursuit of certainty. In: T. Fenwick and R. Edwards, eds., *Researching education through actor-network theory*. Chichester: John Wiley & Sons, pp. 60–77.

Grant, A., Kinnersley, P. and Field, M. (2012). Learning contexts at two UK medical schools: A comparative study using mixed methods. *BMC Research Notes*, 5(153).

Hager, P., Lee, A. and Reich, A. (2012). Problematising practice, reconceptualising learning and imagining change. In: P. Hager, A. Lee and A. Reich, eds., *Practice, learning and change: Practice-theory perspectives on professional learning.* Dordrecht: Springer, pp. 1–14.

Holden, R.J., Carayon, P., Gurses, A.P., Hoonakker, P., Hundt, A.S., Ozok, A.A. and Rivera-Rodriguez, A.J. (2013). SEIPS 2.0: A human factors framework for studying and improving the work of healthcare professionals and patients. *Ergonomics*, 56(11), pp. 1669–1686.

Ibrahim, E.F., Richardson, M.D. and Nestel, D. (2015). Mental imagery and learning: A qualitative study in orthopaedic trauma surgery. *Medical Education*, 49(9), pp. 888–900.

The Institute for Healthcare Improvement. (2017). *Open school. IHI open school online courses: Quality improvement practicum.* Available at: www.ihi.org/education/ IHIOpenSchool/ Courses/Pages/Practicum.aspx [Accessed 11 Nov. 2017].

James, B., Beattie, M., Shepherd, A., Armstrong, L. and Wilkinson, J. (2016). Time, fear and transformation: Student nurses' experiences of doing a practicum (quality improvement project) in practice. *Nurse Education in Practice*, 19, pp. 70–78.

Kuper, A., Whitehead, C. and Hodges, B.D. (2013). Looking back to move forward: Using history, discourse and text in medical education research: AMEE Guide No. 73. *Medical Teacher*, 35(1), pp. e849–e860.

Landri, P. (2012). A return to practice: Practice-based studies of education. In: P. Hager, A. Lee and A. Reich, eds., *Practice, learning and change: Practice-theory perspectives on professional learning.* Dordrecht: Springer, pp. 85–100.

Langley, G.J., Moen, R.D., Nolan, K.M., Nolan, T.W., Norman, C.L. and Provost, L.P. (2009). *The improvement guide: A practical approach to enhancing organizational performance.* 2nd ed. San Francisco, CA: Jossey-Bass.

Latour, B. (1987). *Science in action: How to follow scientists and engineers through society.* Cambridge, MA: Harvard University Press.

Latour, B. (1999). On recalling ANT. In: J. Law and J. Hassard, eds., *Actor network theory and after.* Oxford: Blackwell Publishing, pp. 15–25.

Latour, B. and Porter, C. (1996). *Aramis, or, the love of technology.* Cambridge, MA: Harvard University Press.

Latour, B. and Woolgar, S. (2013). *Laboratory life: The construction of scientific facts.* Princeton, NJ: Princeton University Press.

Lave, J. and Wenger, E. (1991). *Situated learning: Legitimate peripheral participation.* Cambridge: Cambridge University Press.

Law, J. and Singleton, V. (2003). Allegory and its others. In: D. Nicolini, S. Gherardi and D. Yanow, eds., *Knowing in organizations: A practice-based approach.* Armonk, NY: M.E. Sharpe, pp. 225–254.

Lindsay, B. (2007). *Understanding research and evidence-based practice.* Exeter: Reflect Press.

Lucas, B. and Nacer, H. (2015). *The habits of an improver: Thinking about learning for improvement in healthcare.* Discussion Paper. London: The Health Foundation.

McKimm, J., Forrest, K. and Thistlethwaite, J. (2017). *Medical education at a glance.* Chichester: John Wiley & Sons.

McMurtry, A., Rohse, S. and Kilgour, K.N. (2016). Socio-material perspectives on interprofessional team and collaborative learning. *Medical Education*, 50(2), pp. 169–180.

Mitchell, B. (2020). Student-led improvement science projects: A praxiographic, actor-network theory study. *Studies in Continuing Education*, 42(1), pp. 133–146.

Mitchell, B., Cristancho, S., Nyhof, B.B. and Lingard, L.A. (2017). Mobilising or standing still? A narrative review of surgical safety checklist knowledge as developed in 25 highly cited papers from 2009 to 2016. *BMJ Quality & Safety*, 26(10).

Mol, A. (2002). *The body multiple: Ontology in medical practice*. Durham: Duke University Press.

Mulcahy, D. (2014). Re-thinking teacher professional learning: More than a representational account. In: T. Fenwick and M. Nerland, eds., *Reconceptualising professional learning: Sociomaterial knowledges, practices and responsibilities*. Abingdon: Routledge, pp. 52–66.

Nespor, J. (2012). Devices and educational change. In: T. Fenwick and R. Edwards, eds., *Researching education through actor-network theory*. Chichester: John Wiley & Sons, pp. 1–22.

Nespor, J. (2014). *Knowledge in motion: Space, time and curriculum in undergraduate physics and management*. Abingdon: Routledge.

Okwemba, S. and Copeland, L. (2014). Improving mental status questionnaire (MSQ) completion on admission to the acute surgical receiving unit (ASRU), Ninewells Hospital, Dundee. *BMJ Quality Improvement Reports*, 3(1), u205217–w2159.

Paterson, G., Rossi, J., MacLean, S., Dolan, R., Johnston, T., Linden, D., Arbuckle, S., Lynch, N. and Davey, P. (2011). A patient safety 'student selected component' at the university of Dundee (UK). *International Journal of Clinical Skills*, 5(2).

Peden, C. and Rooney, K. (2009). The science of improvement as it relates to quality and safety in the ICU. *Journal of the Intensive Care Society*, 10(4), pp. 260–264.

Price, O.M., Johnsson, M.C., Scheeres, H., Boud, D. and Solomon, N. (2012). Learning organizational practices that persist, perpetuate and change: A Schatzkian view. In: P. Hager, A. Lee and A. Reich, eds. *Practice, learning and change: Practice-theory perspectives on professional learning*. Dordrecht: Springer, pp. 233–247.

Roberts, J. (2006). Limits to communities of practice. *Journal of Management Studies*, 43(3), pp. 623–639.

Rowe, A. and Chapman, C. (2015). *Perspectives on improvement and effectiveness: Key definitions and concepts*. Edinburgh: What Works Scotland. Available at: http://whatworksscotland.ac.uk/wp-content/uploads/2015/11/Perspectives-on-Improvement.pdf [Accessed 11 Nov. 2017].

Sørensen, E. (2009). *The materiality of learning: Technology and knowledge in educational practice*. Cambridge: Cambridge University Press.

Star, S.L. (1990). Power, technology and the phenomenology of conventions: On being allergic to onions. *The Sociological Review*, 38 (suppl 1), pp. 26–56.

University of Stirling, Department of Health Sciences (2015). *Advanced practice masters degree*. Available at: www.stir.ac.uk/postgraduate/programme-information/prospectus/health-sciences/advanced-practice/ [Accessed 11 Nov. 2017].

Verran, H. (2001). *Science and an African logic*. Chicago, IL: University of Chicago Press.

Wong, B.M., Etchells, E.E., Kuper, A., Levinson, W. and Shojania, K.G. (2010). Teaching quality improvement and patient safety to trainees: A systematic review. *Academic Medicine: Journal of the Association of American Medical Colleges*, 85(9), pp. 1425–1439.

Zukas, M. and Kilminster, S. (2012). Learning to practise, practising to learn: Doctors' transitions to new levels of responsibility. In: P. Hager, A. Lee and A. Reich, eds. *Practice, learning and change: Practice-theory perspectives on professional learning*. Dordrecht: Springer, pp. 199–213.

Zukas, M. and Kilminster, S. (2014). The doctor and the blue form: Learning professional responsibility. In: T. Fenwick and M. Nerland, eds., *Reconceptualising professional learning: Sociomaterial knowledges, practices and responsibilities*. Abingdon: Routledge, pp. 38–51.

Chapter 4

The research assemblage

This chapter introduces the empirical study of SLISPs in a hospital setting and outlines the research strategy in relation to the theoretical orientation of ANT and education. The chapter is split into two parts. In Part 1, the methodology is outlined by describing socio-materiality and ANT as derived from practice and professional education. Part 1 goes on to outline the strategies taken to ensure rigour and validity in empirical ANT research, and the associated problems. Part 2 describes the research design and provides an overview of the analysis and how this was carried out. This part also describes how the fieldwork was set up, including the initial meetings and the ethics process. The two cohorts and their associated SLISPs are then introduced. There is a focus on the different types of information collected in the field, such as documents, interviews, fieldnotes, and photographs. The specific ANT concepts of networks, symmetry, and multiple worlds are revisited in relation to the analytical strategy in light of preliminary data that was collected.

Part 1: Ontological orientation of the analysis

According to Martin and Kamberelis (2013), positivism and post-positivism remain the most dominant approaches in education research. In positivist ontology, the researcher strives to be objective; the assumption is that there is a 'real truth' out there for the researcher to discover, with its own inherent meaning. In education, positivist approaches are used to measure performance, and positivism is a dominant approach in medical education research and improvement science; but this can be problematic. For example, in the classroom, observed behaviours are subject to interpretation, which cannot be adequately explored through positivist approaches (Pring and Thomas, 2004). It is becoming more widely accepted in medical research that a positivist stance is not always appropriate to reflect the nuance of social and material interactions. For example, a recent open letter to The BMJ calls for more qualitative studies in the medical literature (Greenhalgh et al., 2016).

Research based on positivist values presents an ontological position where 'phenomenological experience . . . is assumed to be essential, stable, and universal' (Martin and Kamberelis, 2013, p. 670). In the analysis of work-place practice, essentialism and universality can be problematic and engenders research approaches based on assumptions of a reality that is 'out there' (Law, 2004). As an alternative, Martin and Kamberelis (2013) suggest an approach to analysis that is more like mapping, which accommodates open and unpredictable systems more suitable for studying practice. In other words, an approach to the data that creates new paths rather than tracing existing ones. Mapping may be more suited to post-structural approaches that are required to open out concepts rather than closing down into categories. For example, grounded theory may be considered to have a convergent trajectory by continually grouping data into codes and categorisations (Denzin and Lincoln, 2005). In contrast, ANT could be said to have a divergent analytic trajectory, where the object of inquiry is constantly interrupted and intervened to challenge its status as a singularity. The aim of grounded theory is to condense, and the difficulty of this strategy is knowing how to group things together. The aim of ANT is to disperse, and the difficulty of this strategy is knowing where to stop, or where to 'cut the network' (Fenwick, Edwards and Sawchuk, 2011). Fenwick, Edwards and Sawchuk (2011) describe ANT as striving to represent complexity, and not to 'iron out the wrinkles' to present a flat, linear representation of the fieldwork. Law (2004) describes 'looking down' into the detail of practices rather than 'looking up' at overarching structures; the curlicues of the Baroque as opposed to the weightless dreams of the Romantic. Mol (2002) presents the idea of 'praxiography', a form of ethnography, as a way of exploring uncertainty without closing down complex ideas by explaining phenomena. The strategy for this analysis is therefore mapping new paths through the data, through inquiry and questioning. The concepts of networks and praxiography are explored in more detail later in this chapter, and outlined in a paper describing this study (Mitchell, 2020).

The research in this book has taken the socio-material position of ANT by considering knowledge and learning in space/time: 'It is in these organisations of space and time that we will find the key to understanding how students "learn" in fields of "knowledge"' (Nespor, 2014, p. 16). When knowledge and learning are considered in this way, the notion of measurement becomes elusive and requires a different set of research strategies to measuring knowledge and learning as static and reified. In a workplace environment, practice is not necessarily individualised and cannot be easily separated into isolated components. In other words, it can be difficult for an observer to separate the work of an individual when they are working in clinical teams and carrying out different processes that overlap. The implications of considering knowledge and learning as social, situated and material are that relational effects become entangled and contingent (Landri, 2012). In medical education, this reconceptualisation requires a different way of thinking about educative approaches. In many ways, socio-material approaches are more aligned to the mess and complexity of the hospital ward than more traditional approaches that measure and assess separate components. For a socio-material approach, the researcher is required to notice how materials (bodies, documents, equipment, furniture) and social dynamics (meanings, decisions, interactions) are enmeshed, allowing taken-for-granted or hidden forces to be made visible (Fenwick and Nimmo, 2015).

The aim of the research described in this book was to conduct an analysis drawing from an ANT sensibility, which is non-representative, divergent and exploratory. To achieve this, I started by identifying some of the guiding principles of ANT that I felt would be helpful for the analysis. My decisions were based on the literature, particularly drawing from empirical studies in ANT (Latour, 1987, 1999a; Latour and Porter, 1996; Latour and Woolgar, 2013), ANT and education (Nespor, 2014; Sørensen, 2009) and ANT and healthcare (Law and Singleton, 2000; Law and Singleton, 2003; Mol, 2002). These studies were helpful for practical considerations, as well as demonstrating how the authors had drawn together ANT with ethnography in the field and subsequent analysis. I closely followed literature that drew together central issues of ANT in education research (Fenwick and Edwards, 2010), ANT in medical education (Bleakley, Bligh and Browne, 2011) and the development of classic ANT to after-ANT (Latour, 1999b; Latour, 2005; Law and Hassard, 1999; Mol, 1998). I first turned to Latour (2005), Nespor (2014) and Sørensen (2009) for their descriptions of networks and how these were presented empirically. The concept of networks is described in the next section. Although the network metaphor helped me to navigate through my fieldwork and analysis, I felt that more could be drawn from ANT. Because so much had been written about the concept of symmetry in ANT, especially in the critiques, I felt this needed to be addressed as a perspective in my research. I drew from Law (2004) and Mol (2002) for more after-ANT developments relating to analytical methods to explore SLISPs.

Guiding concepts from actor-network theory

There are many tools and concepts that ANT affords, coming from different authors, traditions and times. For example, Callon's 'four moments of translation' describe different ways in which networks become stabilised in practice: through 'problematisation' and how the problem is framed; 'interessment' or how entities assemble or are excluded; 'enrollment' of actors into the network; and 'mobilisation' through stabilisation of a network (Callon, 1984). There are examples of ANT analyses in education that draw from the four moments of translation (Nespor, 2014; Sørensen, 2009; Zukas and Kilminster, 2014). Although this approach has proved to be fruitful, I elected not to apply this framework as I wanted to develop my own methodology that would also include more recent developments in ANT. Other ANT studies in education focus on specific features; for example, Edwards, Biesta and Thorpe (2009) place a focus on the concept of 'tokens', referring to objects or discourses that are continuously translated and changed as they move through space and time.

Fenwick (2009) draws from notions arising through the after-ANT movement to 'appreciate the spaces or blanks beyond networks' (Fenwick, 2009, p. 98).

In my approach, I have concentrated on three specific ANT concepts to guide the analysis: networks, symmetry, and multiple worlds, as these are the prominent methodologies in ANT which attend to recent theoretical developments. I adapted these three dimensions from a list of five (Fenwick and Edwards, 2010) as a way of drawing out more mature ANT concepts (networks and symmetry) and more recent, after-ANT ideas (multiple worlds). These three dimensions are not discrete and there is overlap. However, I have treated these as a way to focus on facets of the research, to draw out insights that will address the research questions. My research aim was to investigate student learning during the process of carrying out SLISPs. My theoretical orientation conceptualises learning as a network effect which is dynamic and contingent. To explore this aim, my research probed the network effects that were produced during the projects, and what observable practices were recordable. A focus on networks was necessary to answer these questions, but introducing other ANT concepts provides alternative descriptions that move the data in a different way.

Networks

The metaphor of networks has been referred to in many empirical and theoretical ANT studies, and has been related to knowledge and learning: 'knowledge is generated through the process and effects of these assemblages coming together . . . learning itself becomes enacted as a network effect' (Fenwick and Edwards, 2010, p. 4). Nespor's (2014) study on the networks of physics and management in higher education has been very influential for situating knowledge in space/time, and for developing a terminology to support this by describing the differences between networks of physics and management courses (Fenwick, Edwards and Sawchuk, 2011). Sørensen's (2009) The Materiality of Learning is a detailed examination of education practices drawing from ANT. Sørensen describes the research as 'a development from being entangled in one network to becoming entangled in another – a spatial movement rather than a temporal progression' (Sørensen, 2009, p. 73).

Although the enactment of the network's metaphor has helped to reconceptualise learning and knowledge in new and interesting ways, it has also raised a number of issues. I have identified four main points of concern about networks. First, the network is dynamic and conceptual, as opposed to being a fixed and transportable framework. Latour (2005) identifies the 'new' use of the term network as having divorced itself from ideas such as rail systems or computer networks. Instead, the word 'network' is used to describe the translations and effects that take place when elements come together (Latour, 1999b). The second point is to do with the role of the researcher. As someone who is not participating in the 'world' of the network, I cannot represent the network, either as an insider or an outsider. The third point is related to the second, because in early applications of ANT there was a danger of attempting to represent only the most powerful or visible actors. The last point is that everything the researcher sees is included in the network, at the exclusion of some entities: 'the temptation to collapse all interactions and connections into networks needs to be avoided . . . not all relations that contribute to producing these effects will be networks' (Fenwick and Edwards, 2012, p. xviii). In other words, the network becomes everything the researcher considers to be in the network, with other elements being disregarded, which is why the researcher speaking for the world is problematic and why representation is avoided. During my fieldwork, I experienced how I became part of different networks, as connections strengthened through being involved in situations. For example, I was considered part of the project group for the second cohort, as I worked alongside the students at all times.

I therefore draw from the concept of networks whilst considering these potential problems. My research explores SLISPs as situated, practice-based, and entwined, from which learning emerges through network effects (Ahn et al., 2015). The main advantages of conceptualising networks are as a way of describing relations between entities rather than the entities themselves, and observing how networks interact through strengthening connections to become more stable or by weakening the forces that hold networks together. Another advantage is to view everything as potentially affecting the network through forces and relations; the entities themselves are not considered unless they act upon the network (Latour, 2005).

Symmetry

Symmetry describes how dualisms are challenged in ANT; for example, humans are not foregrounded in favour of non-humans, as commonly happens in sociological theory. As previously described, ANT looks at networks and relations, at associations between entities rather than bounded individual entities. This raises questions about how the researcher (a human) presents non-humans and also about how non-humans participate in the social (McLean and Hassard, 2004). An ANT sensibility considers what things do rather than what they are; what effects elements have within their particular networks and what associations are formed. In terms of how knowledge is conceptualised:

> knowing, or coming to know something, is regarded as something that emerges as an effect of the socio-material arrangements that gather together and are performed into being through the continual transactions.
>
> (Ahn et al., 2015)

In this way, ANT is different from other forms of enquiry, as elements of the network only exist as associations with other entities within that network;

in another network, they might have different effects and perform different realities. For example, during my fieldwork I observed a student looking at medical notes that had been filled out with a thick, italic pen. Numbers were illegible because of the thickness of the pen and information was obscured. In the second cohort, it was noted that pharmacists use a green pen, so evidence of pharmacists writing notes was plain to see. In both cases, the pen in each network created an effect that would have been different in other networks. For example, the thick, italic pen would have a different effect if it was used for writing a sign: a thicker mark would be more noticeable and more likely to shape actions; and the green pen used by the pharmacist would not have the same associations in a different network. Focusing on the pen itself might not have provided these insights, but understanding what the pen performed within the network, and the practices it then shaped, provided a better understanding of effects and interactions.

Multiple ontologies

Bleakley (2012) describes ANT as a research practice that challenges conventional evidence in medical education by exploring multiple possibilities rather than a singular meaning. He describes multiple worlds in relation to networks:

> ANT is interested primarily not in epistemologies, but in how a phenomenon such as an 'illness' is conceived across differing practices as multiple ontologies (experienced meanings), each meaning generated and suspended within a particular network of effects. How such networks are initiated and developed has significance for rethinking the nature of 'evidence', restoring faith in the value of a good story.
>
> (Bleakley, 2012, p. 462)

Developing the idea that practice networks produce reality, Law (2004) suggests that these different realities can be viewed as different worlds. The conditions of possibility that exist within an ontology are shaped by intervention and performance (Mol, 1998). By focusing on the 'world' produced by practice, the researcher can appreciate the particular rather than the general, can attune to the relations and practices within it and develop a sensibility within that world (Law, 2004). This is a departure from the idea of a 'singular' reality that is behind most health research. As mentioned earlier, Bleakley (2012) describes multiple ontologies as performing the opposite function to triangulation: instead of focusing different perspectives on a single object, the object is allowed to open out into how it would perform in different worlds and become a multiplicity.

Mol (1998) presents the concept of 'multiple ontologies' to describe how, within the multiple possibilities within a world, choices and decisions are made. If one accepts the idea of multiple worlds, then there needs to be some consideration regarding how these worlds coexist or compete. Alongside the concept of symmetry, where the object/subject, nature/society, and human/ non-human dichotomies are eschewed, the interactions of multiple worlds draw out differences in new ways. Star (1990) asks 'cui bono?' or 'who stands to gain?', and Mol (1998) asks, 'what is at stake?' to explore what is excluded when the hierarchy of a situation is flattened by taking privilege away from humans over non-humans, or foregrounding what are perceived as more important actors. In other words, ontological politics is the examination of what is focused on in a situation and what is ignored. Mol (1998) also distinguishes between plurality and multiplicity. Plurality refers to many things, but multiplicity means the opening up of a thing, so it is between one and many. For example, a single medical form enacts multiple practices, but there are many medical forms on the ward. Fenwick, Edwards and Sawchuk (2011) put forward the possible implications of considering multiple worlds as presenting questions regarding how worlds are conceptualised and treated.

By drawing from the concept of multiple worlds it was possible to trace how different practices interrelated, and how different associations of the same entity produced different effects. This is relevant to the study of improvement science practices in SLISPs in relation to medical practices such as antimicrobial prescribing and insulin recording. Rather than referring to the practices as different contexts for SLISPs, the concept of multiple worlds allows for these boundaries to be challenged and broken down, and to consider a more relational, ecological view where practices are enmeshed, situated, and contingent. This was achieved in this research through exploring difference and ambiguity, which would sometimes signpost to a multiple; for example, Mol (2002) describes how atherosclerosis is performed into being in multiple ways, rather than existing a reified, singular condition.

Ethnography and praxiography

There are many other ways in which this research project could have been carried out, each carrying a set of assumptions and a defined scope. It would have been possible to conduct an ethnography on SLISPs without drawing from ANT, and this would still provide insights into learning. With more recent developments in the field of ethnography, the researcher is now required to consider a more participatory role and to shift the balance of power to the communities they observe, which would have allowed for the type of ethnography carried out in this study (Angrosino, 2007). Angrosino and Rosenberg (2011) also challenge the classic tradition of data gathering through observation. For example, traditional methods strived to standardise data gathering and sampling, whereas more contemporary approaches challenge assumptions of truth and the relationship between the researcher and the researched. They also point out the technological advances that widen the scope of observation and data collection. However, ANT was considered to be intrinsic to the project.

The fieldwork was planned and designed with ANT, and then drawn through in the analysis. The effect of this was to attune to and notice mundane details of fine-grained practice as SLISPs were carried out (Fenwick and Edwards, 2010). More accurately, a praxiographic approach was followed, whereby ambiguities were explored rather than explained (Mol, 2002). As with many ANT studies, this level of detail was best served by a case-study approach (Flyvbjerg, 2011; Kanger, 2017; Stake, 2013). Besides following case study, ethnography, and praxiography, there is no set method or framework to follow for an ANT study. Adams and Thompson (2016) have published a set of heuristics that relate to post-humanism and ANT-related studies. These consist of questions to ask at various stages of research, but are designed to guide rather than instruct. The detail that is required for an ANT study means that a very small part of the picture is blown up and investigated in detail. ANT is non-representational (Latour, 2005), and therefore not a suitable approach to make generalisations.

Rigour and validity in ANT

Qualitative research methods usually result in amassing large amounts of data, such as tens of thousands of words from interview transcripts, fieldnotes, reflective notes, photographs and documents (Anzul et al. 1991; Punch, 2012). The researcher is required to make decisions as to what data is relevant to the research questions, and to undertake processes to present this (Anzul et al., 1991). Developing an analysis strategy from ANT requires the researcher to not only make sense of the data and to be reflexive in their approach to this, but also to interrupt patterns and meaning to hold ideas open. The emphasis is on enactment rather than essentialism; in other words, 'ANT focuses not on what texts and other objects mean, but on what they do' (Fenwick, Edwards and Sawchuk, 2011). In this study the emphasis is on doing and describing, rather than on representing the data to draw out its meaning. When interviews are carried out, many approaches seek to interpret the meaning behind words. However, Latour (2005, p. 49) warns against seeking meaning in an ANT analysis:

> When a criminal says, 'It is not my fault, I had bad parents', should we say that 'society made her a criminal' or that 'she is trying to escape her own personal culpability by diluting it in the anonymity of society' . . . the criminal said nothing of the sort. She simply said 'I had bad parents'.

In relation to ethnographic approaches, Latour and Woolgar (2013) borrow from Harris (1976) the idea of validation through etic and emic approaches. Etic approaches involve using a theory to deduce phenomenon and carrying out empirical research to 'prove' the theory; in this case, validation comes from fellow researchers through categorisation and generalisation. Emic approaches require a longer period for observation, to allow for insights to emerge, which are validated by the participants themselves. In my analysis, an emic approach was followed as it is important that participants validate the research and that insights come from within rather than being imposed by the researcher. This requires careful consideration of what is knowable in a situation, as the ontological position of ANT is not to discover a pre-existing truth but to allow participants to describe their own reality rather than being represented by the researcher. This position is different to the materialisms of, for example, Marx and Engels, which relied upon knowing 'real' people as they 'really are' (Harris, 1976, p. 330). For ANT, participants are considered as assemblages of human and non-human entities whose realities are contingent to the networks they are connected to and the worlds they reside in.

With these analytic preferences stated, it should be noted that many researchers have encountered methodological problems in ANT studies. For example, Nespor (2014) describes, at the end of his account of knowledge and learning in physics and management programmes, how he reconciled the outcomes of his research with what he intended at the outset. He describes the compromises he had to make during the analysis process:

> I gave up some of the mobility, stability, and combinality of the interview discourse by reproducing it in lengthy, relatively immobile chunks that are unstable (in the sense that they allow alternative explications), and mix poorly because they are uncoded.
>
> (Nespor, 2014, p. 153)

Nespor (2014) goes on to say that he expected some degree of reductionism, because there are multiple perspectives that will be mapped over each other to produce a single explanation of what it all means.

I employed ethnographic methods in my research to investigate knowledge and learning through networks, following Latour and Woolgar (2013), Nespor (2014), Mol (2002) and Law (2004). As these authors point out, ethnographic methods originate from the study of people and culture; a sensibility of relations, materialities and networks need to be taken into account for ANT. Bleakley (2014) also points out that an ANT ethnography requires 'special qualities' of the researcher to notice and attend closely to detail. Attending to detail enables a more critical examination that can challenge assumptions and uncover practices that may be less visible or less valued (Law, 2004).

In many research methods, there is a framework to test against or a set of steps to provide guidance, and some are more directive than others. For example, CHAT has a series of stages: model the situation, produce an activity system, decompose this, generate research questions, conduct the investigation, interpret the findings; there is also another system for analysis and the triangle model (Engeström, 2001). In critical discourse analysis, the framework produced by Fairclough can be used to analyse the texts and provides a series of stages (Fairclough, 2003). ANT is not conducive to frameworks that might impose external or theoretical meaning onto a situation. As Latour wrote in a fictional dialogue with a student who was insistent about 'using' ANT as a 'framework':

> 'My Kingdom for a frame!' Very moving; I think I understand your des-peration. But no, ANT is pretty useless for that. Its main tenet is that the actors themselves make everything, including their own frames, their own theories, their own contexts, their own metaphysics, even their own ontologies. So the direction to follow would be more descriptions I am afraid.
>
> (Latour, 2005, p. 147)

Despite this, Bleakley (2011) refers to ANT as a framework, and a recent paper (Kanger, 2017) also puts forward ANT as a framework. In a similar way, the debate about ANT as a theory has been played out in many discussions (Latour, 1999b; Law and Hassard, 1999; Mol, 2010). Adams and Thompson's (2016) set of heuristics are intended as guidance, where not all of them need to be applied, rather than a set of stages to follow in sequence. It would have been incongru-ent with an ANT approach to apply a rigid template, model, or series of steps to be followed. As Law and Singleton (2003) found when they attempted to produce a formatted 'process diagram', practices do not always conform to such treatment, and such handling can lead to a reductive representation of the data. In the absence of a framework or a set of steps, I needed to demonstrate validity and rigour in a different way by forming my own process of analysis.

A dancer's aside

During my research, I worked as a dance instructor. My experience of dance helped to shape my approach to the research. Initially, the styles of dance I prac-ticed (Modern Egyptian and Raqs Sharki) helped me to conceptualise different approaches in research. Commitment to a particular style does not necessarily exclude certain movements that belong to other styles, but there is a need to develop the knowledge of specific styles to know what is congruent and what is not. This is similar to research approaches, in that 'bricolage' allows for different perspectives to come together (Kincheloe, McLaren and Steinberg, 2011), but a knowledge of the ontological roots of different approaches allows the researcher to identify if there is a 'clash'. As Lincoln, Lynham and Guba (2011) argue, some paradigms are commensurable, but not where axioms are contradictory and exclusive, for example, positivist and interpretivist models. In my research I felt the convergent trajectory of coding and categorising, as I had done in the past with grounded theory and Critical Discourse Analysis, was not congruent with the divergent trajectory of ANT. However, this raised its own set of prob-lems. Divergence and difference require an opening out of an already complex set of scenarios, potentially creating inflation and increasing complexity.

This brings me to the second area in which my dance experience came to be helpful. In choreography, the dancer can interpret complex musical pieces but without reducing or increasing the complexity. The dancer 'moves' the music to see it in another way, and presents bodily moves that accentuate some parts of the music but not all. The drum solo in Arabic dance is a good example of this. The dancer does not move a body part to every single beat; some parts of the music are better represented by a pause or by a surprising move that makes the dance interesting but still in keeping with the music. Even so, the dancer considers the whole of the piece and aims to dance in a way that adds to the music, that is, not too simple and repetitious, but also not too busy. In relation to my research, I was not attempting to present an account of my entire research, but to draw out parts that resonated; in this way I could consider all of my data, but not try to put a value on talking about some parts and not others.

Thinking of my analysis in the same way as dance offers me, as a researcher, a way of maintaining complexity without reducing it: 'when we look at dance, we see opportunities for movement, we see obstacles, limitations. We see the world, but we see it as a world-for-movement, that is, the world as a domain for action' (Gehm, Husemann and von Wilcke, 2015, p. 125). In my analysis I have drawn on the experience of building a choreography as a way of maintaining complexity.

Part 2: Research design

I planned to conduct two case studies, referred to as Cohort 1 and Cohort 2. A case study approach allowed for sufficient depth and detail (Flyvbjerg, 2011) in the data to support an overarching ANT methodology. I planned the cases based on the 'quintain' model used in multiple case studies (Stake, 2013). The quintain model helps to consider the boundaries of a case by acknowledging different aspects such as history, setting, policy drivers, and previous research. It also begins to assemble the case by situating the student and the SLISP as the focus of study, rather than focusing solely on the student. This is useful when studying more than one case because similar considerations can be made. I considered the approach to be congruent with ANT as the case became an assemblage of inter-related components rather than focusing on the student or a single actor. Although my research design did not meet the exact criteria of a multiple case study approach as set out by Stake (2013), who recommends this approach for five case studies or more, I found it useful to employ this model for planning. I had originally proposed looking at more cases, but, because I wanted to explore detail and nuance, it was not practical to look at more than two cases. The rationale for two cases was firstly strategic: if one case did not seem to yield enough, or if the case was withdrawn for some reason, then there would be another for contingency. It was not the intention to 'compare and contrast' or to attempt to generalise the outcomes for other SLISPs. However, I found there were unexpected advantages to the research to have more than one case. The main advantage was that it helped to avoid getting too drawn into the SLISP itself and the area of investigation. I found the project topics fascinating, and could see how I might explore the practices directly involved (i.e. antimicrobial stewardship, medical reconciliation, and so on). I found that my focus became more clearly defined throughout the fieldwork period (Ragin and Becker, 1992).

My research took place within a hospital and medical school, where the medical students were enrolled. The other students were pharmacy students from another University.

Before starting the fieldwork with the cohorts, I recorded my own observations of some of the spaces within the hospital. Latour (2005) suggests making lists and keeping different journals for notes relating to different aspects of the research, such as reflections of the researcher. This is for the purpose of making detailed descriptions in the field, which is critical for an ANT investigation. I recorded notes by hand in a spiral-bound, A5 notebook with a margin. I sometimes used the margin to annotate my notes, or sometimes used a pen with a different colour of ink. The materiality of my fieldwork data collection greatly impacted on what I recorded. I invested in a keyboard for my iPad so that I could record additional notes onto Evernote. I have used Evernote throughout my PhD, and I now have an extensive record of my rationale, reasoning and reflections throughout the whole fieldwork process. It is problematic to separate these notes as 'reflections', as these are also the start of my analysis through thinking and writing (Crang, 2003). The healthcare sector has a tradition of encouraging reflection as a learning technique but, as Fenwick (2014) warns, this approach assumes that thinking through reflection is separate to doing in practice. My ontological position viewed reflection as entangled with other research activities. However, I do refer to reflection in the notes as a way of indicating that these notes were made after observations and interviews.

It would be easy to exclude or demote my notes on Evernote as these were not a record of what I saw and heard but of what I felt and reacted, which I considered to be an important part of the research process. However, these notes can lead to surprising connections and insights into the data (Crang, 2003). Punch (2012) draws extensively from a reflective diary in her experiences of conducting an ethnography in Bolivia. She describes these as an intrinsic part of fieldwork that can sometimes be made invisible in ethnographies. I also used Evernote to record things I could not write down at the time:

> Reflecting on the observation yesterday, there were a couple of things I didn't write down (I didn't want anyone to see!) These were the story about the SR [Specialist Registrar] who asked me if I was a medical student and I said no . . . Later [medical student] said we had to hide because they'd be on the look-out for students to take samples, so that might've been why he asked.

As the above extract shows, keeping separate notes was sometimes necessary, as it would sometimes have been inappropriate or insensitive to share my thoughts with staff who were not familiar with my study. In this example, there was a practical reason for writing notes after the event. The Specialist Registrar, mentioned in the extract, had asked me if I was a medical student and I was puzzled by the reason for his question. I responded by telling him that I was a social science researcher and asked if he wanted me to leave; I was observing a ward round with a crowd of clinical staff and assumed I was in the way. The Registrar was happy for me to stay and made it clear that this was not the reason for the question. It was only after the incident that the student I was observing told me that it was common on ward round to be asked to participate by, for example, taking blood samples. This was considered to be an opportunity for medical students to gain experience. The student had suggested that we 'hide' to avoid being asked to participate as we were observing other activities. The example also highlights my participation as an observer and the way my presence created network effects; I was entangled in the situation. As Barad (2007) would say, I was intra-acting as a co-producer of reality rather than inter-acting without producing effects.

Hammersley (1993) described making notes away from the situation when it felt inappropriate to write in front of participants, and how he made frequent excuses to go to the toilet to do this. Fox (1990) detailed his embarrassment when a participant forcefully took his notes during an observation and ridiculed the notes in front of other participants. These examples illustrate the potential difficulties with making notes in the field, and how the researcher needs to use their discretion to decide the potential impact of this. My Evernote notes helped me to record and recall the detail of specific situations very soon after they occurred. The process of making notes before and after observations was very useful to me in the field. Evernote helped me to debrief after spending time at the hospital, and provided a journal record as the fieldwork progressed.

Cohort I SLISP: antimicrobial prescribing

I began my fieldwork by formally interviewing a medical student. The purpose of the interview was to gain a better understanding of SLISPs and their project in particular. I anticipated that this would help me to plan the observations and ethnography, to make the best use of time on the hospital wards. The initial interview helped to build trust with the student and enabled me to become more familiar with what they would be attending to as they carried out work for their SLISP. I made the decision to fully transcribe all my interviews. My decision was based on past experience of partial transcriptions, which I felt were not adequate for the kind of analysis I was applying; in order to transcribe only 'relevant' sections, I had to first decide what was 'relevant' and I needed to be very familiar with my data before I could do this. I fully transcribed the recordings in terms of typing every word, but without including pauses, emphasis, gestures, and so on, as might be carried out in conversation analysis. I typed the transcriptions onto a word document and printed off hard copies. I experimented with methods to analyse the interviews as I wanted to connect the interviews to the fieldwork and to the examples I used in the analysis. I used post-it notes on the hard copies to indicate information that I referred to in the analysis. I also used the 'Track Changes' function in Word to mark the documents electronically; I found that it was easier to analyse the transcripts electronically as it was easier to search the documents. I used the 'Comments' function to annotate the transcripts and to highlight sections that linked to the fieldwork. I also experimented with mind-mapping to analyse the interview recordings.

Cohort 1's SLISP was about antimicrobial prescribing as part of a wider project in quality improvement. The student, as part of the SLISP, became my first case, which I refer to as Cohort 1. I accompanied the student to investigate the most suitable wards for study, and met with consultants and other staff to discuss how the study would be carried out. The student decided to conduct the SLISP in two wards. After the wards were selected, I conducted my own observations alone, to attune to the environment. On one occasion I was turned away from a ward as the senior charge nurse felt the ward was too busy at the time. I found that my presence was more accepted when I accompanied the student than when I was alone. However, my solo observations proved to be very illuminating and important for the study. I also accompanied the student to observe meetings and events such as creative workshops to promote research and improvement methods.

Cohort 2 SLISP: insulin recording

The second case was a SLISP project undertaken by a group, comprising a medical student and two pharmacy students from another university. The focus of their SLISP project was improving medical reconciliation for insulin-dependent patients. I made the decision, through discussion with my supervisors, to include all three students rather than to 'pick' one student and to review this as the project progressed. My rationale was that it might be awkward to focus on one student when the three students were working together on the project. I was also conscious of the short timescale; the project was for four weeks in total, so the students would need to be focused on their project for the time they were together, and having a researcher asking questions of only one of the students might inconvenience them and put them at a disadvantage. My decision to work with all three students meant that I could keep closer to the practices of the project and use my discretion as to what I was observing and who I was speaking to.

At the start, the students had a discussion with their allocated clinical team about where to situate their study. They decided on two wards. These were very similar to the wards studied by Cohort 1 in terms of working practices.

One of the wards was slightly different in that it was busier, and the rotation of Foundation Year (FY) doctors was much more rapid (a few days as opposed to a few months). This had consequences for the project, as staff engagement, opinion and 'buy-in' was critical to the uptake of the improvement. This was particularly true for FY doctors as they would be more likely to fill out the medical reconciliation forms that the students were proposing to change.

My work with Cohort 2 involved being with the group as they visited wards and also carried out their project in other spaces. This was because the wards were busy and open, and we needed to be sensitive to working staff. I decided whether to accompany students on the wards based on whether I thought I might get in the way and hinder the project. I also respected the wishes of the group when they suggested visiting the wards alone or in smaller numbers, being mindful of the impact we might have on the ward. The group spent time on the project in other spaces such as the rest area, teaching rooms, the computer room at the library, pharmacy offices, and the locker room.

I interviewed the students as a group initially, then individually. It was difficult to allocate time towards interviews, as time on the project was limited. The initial group meeting was opportunistic as I had been unable to fix a time to interview the students separately. The students had little time to get to know each other and to decide how they would carry out the project, and I exercised my discretion as a researcher to ensure their needs were prioritised. Later in the project I was able to interview the students individually. After the project had finished, I interviewed another key contact who was named by the students. The group set up an online chat facility, which they agreed I could include in my research. This proved to be very useful for tracking dates of particular incidents during the project. I also took photographs and collected documents. The documents I collected for both cohorts were blank medical forms and documents relating to the SLISP projects. The photographs I took with Cohort 1 were noticeably different from the photographs in Cohort 2. In Cohort 1, I was given permission to photograph Ward 1 as, being in side rooms, the patients could not be seen. I ensured any identifying information was blanked out. In Cohort 2, I took pictures of practices outside the ward, for example handling forms in the rest area and in the locker room. I later made collages of the two cohorts, and the different content of the photographs created contrasting images. As mentioned earlier, the cohorts were not intended to be compared, but it was interesting to see how the configuration of the photographs gave each cohort a different character.

Attuning to the hospital environment

My early notes capture the feelings I had of being in the hospital. This helped me to reflect on my role as a researcher and to position myself in the working environment. Starting the observations on my own also helped me to make decisions on where to record notes. I used handwritten notes during observations, and typed reflective notes into Evernote, sometimes when I was travelling home on the train. In one account of a solo observation, a nurse from a different ward comes in and I realise for the first time that even people who work in the hospital can feel out of place, as I did:

> A visiting nurse doesn't realise she's in the way, apologises, and dashes out of the way for the bed to get past. I'm glad I'm not the only one!

At the start of my fieldwork, my greatest worry was being in the way. It was comforting to realise that everyone is in the way at some point, and has moments of awkwardness even if they have a lot of experience in that environment. There are several instances of feeling in the way throughout Cohorts 1 and 2. This started to flag up the connectedness of practices and the strength of existing networks.

I also recorded how the corridors of one of the wards become busy and quiet, and the effect of all the patients being in side rooms:

> At one point, there are lots of people in the corridor, then they are all gone, just like that. The side rooms give the effect of bursts of activity – movement, sound and talk.

At the early stages, it was difficult to know what to attend to, what to sensitise to. It was difficult to analyse this part of my fieldwork, as the SLISP component was not yet at play. However, observing solo allowed me to look at things without understanding the meaning; some of the practices I recorded were beyond my experience and comprehension.

I also made a note in my reflections about not taking notes when my student was talking to people:

> I was a bit overwhelmed . . . I found it difficult to write notes in the beginning because we were walking around and I didn't want to bump into things. I was also trying to pay attention to what was going on, so I didn't take notes whilst [the student] was speaking to staff.

This is another example of intra-action (Barad, 2007) and of being conscious of making connections. It was also an example of how I began to attune to the environment during the fieldwork. From an ethical perspective, I was conscious of the effect of my presence and how this might impact on the SLISP. I constantly had to think about my position and how this affected the project; the Evernote notes helped me to do this.

Different types of data

Throughout my fieldwork, I took notes, collected documents, took photographs and drew diagrams. I recorded interviews and transcribed these. I had planned to collect information in this way, but there were some adjustments that I made as I went along, and I also included some sources that I had not anticipated such as a social media group. I revised my processes from Cohort 1 and applied these to Cohort 2. There were some differences between the two cohorts which meant that the information I collected was different, and therefore my analysis would also be adjusted.

I found the quintain (Stake, 2013) to be a useful way of revising my researcher position in relation to the two cases I was studying. Initially, I found I was becoming entangled in the SLISPs that students were undertaking as I carried out observations. By conducting two cases I was able to focus more on my own research questions. However, the quintain presents the assumption that the boundaries around each case are knowable, but in practice there are a great deal of assumptions (Hassard, Kelemen and Cox, 2012). For example, one of the dimensions of each case was time: Cohort 1 was undertaking a longer-term study which I was only studying part of, whereas Cohort 2 had a clear timebound demarcation, with the group only being together for exactly four weeks. Also, there was the effect my increasing familiarity with some aspects of the hospital over time. Drawing from an example from dance, when action is being observed in an environment (in this case a hospital ward), the observer relies on their perceptions to become acquainted with the environment; in other words, it is difficult to understand what is going on until things become more familiar (Gehm, Husemann and von Wilcke, 2015).

I recorded fieldnotes by hand in a spiral bound notebook. I annotated the notes with a pen with ink of a different colour and marked different days and incidents with post-it notes. At first, I carried two notebooks with me: one for notes with the student and one for my own notes. However, I used my iPad and keyboard to make notes with Evernote, and this became my way of recording reflections. By the end of my fieldwork I had two notebooks for each cohort and reflective notes on Evernote. I conducted my analysis of the fieldnotes in stages. At first, I read through them and followed particular incidents to become more familiar with what I had recorded. I then decided to scan the notes into PDF files. I did this twice, first with a separate file for each observation or meeting, so that I could hyperlink these individually to my fieldwork log. I then made PDF files of the whole books. This allowed me to annotate each book and to be able to search the whole of the book. Although I ended up with the same information in three places (hard copy, separate electronic files, and files of entire books), this allowed me to navigate through each observation separately, and also to search whole books to trace devices or incidents.

As described earlier, I transcribed all of my recordings. Doing this allowed me to trace incidents and devices. I annotated the hard-copies and used post-its to indicate places of relevance. For some transcripts, I annotated notes electronically. It seemed appropriate to use different methods as the interviews themselves were different. The interview analysis summary helped me to keep track of all of the interviews. I compiled my reflective notes from Evernote into

Word documents in date order. This gave me a chronology of the reflections. I also made hyperlinks to individual reflections on the fieldwork log to ensure the reflections were connected to the appropriate observations and interviews. For Cohort 2, I found that the written information extended to social media. I sought permission from the students to include this in my analysis, as I found this to be useful. The Slack group, for example, was a message board for everyone in the project to keep in touch. By the end of the fieldwork, the Slack group provided a chronology of incidents that I could compare to the notes I had taken.

I was permitted to take away blank medical forms from the wards. These were useful to clarify what was being recorded on the forms that my students were looking at. For example, the prescription chart (Kardex) featured prominently for Cohort 1, and contained information such as codes to indicate how the boxes should be filled out. I was given a blank prescription chart for gentamycin, which printed with a red bar and a sticky strip to be attached to the prescription chart. The (pink) insulin forms, including the Insulin Prescription and Diabetes Monitoring Record and the Intravenous Insulin Management Guideline (referred to as the 'sliding scale'), were relevant to Cohort 2's SLISP. The admissions form with the medical reconciliation chart was also useful to look at for both cohorts. I also accessed forms and protocols online from the Formulary. The forms contained detailed information regarding how they are to be completed, and it was useful to be able to read these in detail away from the wards. I was able to photograph the forms as they were used in practice, with the students putting stickers onto blank forms. For Cohort 2, I collected the IHI Open School Practicum documents as they were used: these included the cause and effect, or fishbone, diagram; the process diagram; PDSA cycles; and the reporting forms. These were useful records of the students' project as it progressed.

Visual methods

I experimented with the photographs that I had taken as I continued to analyse the data. At first, I isolated images of some of the materials involved in SLISPs, and mapped these into a 'narrative pathway'. This helped me to attune to connections and associations. The diagrams I then used visual methods to compile the images from each cohort into a photomontage. Latour and Woolgar (2013) used photomontages in Laboratory Life, and visual methods can contribute greatly to analysis (Prosser, 2011). I used these images to help me notice details of each project. Another method of visual analysis I used was by using the 'remove background' function on PowerPoint. This isolated parts of the picture through contrast and brightness; but instead of separating objects and people, the function selected parts of different objects. The images helped me to conceptualise elements of practice as being stuck together (Fenwick, Edwards and Sawchuk, 2011) rather than reduced and compartmentalised into separate objects and people. The process challenged conventional boundaries and prompted me to think about how materials assemble and operate together. Writing descriptions of the data enabled me to analyse situations and to think about the way I articulated workplace practices. The process of de-centring the human in ANT accounts is problematic as language is a human endeavour and objects cannot communicate. Bruni (2005) wrote of a hospital electronic patient record (EPR) system from with the notion of a non-human ethnography. Law and Singleton (2003) described how a process model they had been constructing did not relate to the systems they had observed, and instead described the process through narrative. I used both writing descriptions and constructing images to help with the analysis.

I experimented with collage techniques and animating images on Power-Point to help me to conceptualise networks, and also to allow my analysis to symmetrically consider humans and non-humans. This also helped me to articulate my treatment of elements as associative, situated, interconnected and dynamic. Crang (2003) describes the theorist Walter Benjamin's concepts of conjunction and decontextualisation, taking seemingly mundane information and putting it in a different context to highlight new connections and insights. Benjamin embraced the differences that researchers might detect in the same information rather than trying to 'remove bias' and homogenise the data. Rather than think of analysis as producing something final, it is a 'momentary pause in an endless flow' (Crang, 2003, p. 135). Benjamin saw the collage as disrupting linear arguments in restrictive, linear writing. I found that experimenting with images to produce collages and montages helped me to analyse the data I had collected in a non-linear way that was appropriate for ANT. The idea of montage and collage is aligned with the divergent nature of my analysis and facilitates the opening of data rather than converging and grouping. Collage also helps to think of entities as channels of forces and action rather than metaphysical 'things' with inherent properties. Entities can be conceptualised as conduits of learning, as nodes in the network where knowledge gathers. By considering the texture of practice (Fenwick and Landri, 2012), we sensitise to the feel, smell, sound and noise of it. The visual images are explored further in relation to the ANT dimensions later in this chapter.

Analytical strategy

As emphasised throughout the chapter so far, the ontological orientation of this research required an approach to analysis that was thorough but not rigidly methodical. Adams and Thompson (2016) and Law (2006) suggest asking questions of the data to 'tell stories, stories about noise. Actor-network noise. The kinds of noises made by actor-network theory' (Law, 2006, p. 33).

In my research plan, I had time ring-fenced under 'analysis', but this was referring to the time I had after finishing my fieldwork and before beginning to write up. I knew that these stages were not discrete and there would be lots of overlap. Analysis is not a discrete part of the research process, but something that begins at an undetermined time (Crang, 2003; Silverman, 2000). For example, the reflective notes that I had been collecting during my fieldwork could be viewed as an example of 'writing as research process' (Denzin and Lincoln, 2005) and as a way of shaping this process (Punch, 2012). During and after collecting notes and observations from the field, I returned to the research questions to ask questions of the data. I used my research questions to ask what my data told me about my research area, also what was omitted and what my data could not tell me. For example, my observations were limited to the time I was permitted to be on the wards and with the students, and I was aware that it would not be possible to see everything.

As part of my research strategy, I decided to 'follow the actor' (Fenwick and Edwards, 2010) as a way of attuning to materials during the observation, and later as a way to start analysing the data. The process of following the actor is to follow an entity which attracts attention in order to attune to the relations that occur in practice around the actor (Adams and Thompson, 2016). In my research, I was conscious of not favouring the 'big' actors; this had been criticised as an approach in early-ANT work as it only told of the dominant features and networks, whilst silencing the less prominent (ANT and after). Although I had been conscious of this method before starting my fieldwork, I found it difficult to attune to specific actors and to follow these during observations:

> I have got reams of notes from this morning – it's really difficult to know what to pay attention to. I had decided to follow the actor – and had thought about a file or notes. But that was virtually impossible during the ward round. So what now? Follow the trolley? It's not as easy as it sounds. Some of the trolleys go in rooms, some don't (I think). Maybe that's a starting point. Unlike other wards, everything is mobile in this one because the patients are all in different rooms . . . Perhaps I could look at another ward to see the difference?

The note expresses how I tried to physically follow inanimate objects around the ward, but found that these are static for long periods of time. A later idea helped me to focus on the gentamycin form:

> Maybe I could follow an antibiotic prescription from beginning to end? E.g. gentamycin? Then I would have a better perspective on the process.

Following the gentamycin form for me was about following numerous forms over time. As I continued with the observations, I noticed the gentamycin form, but it was not until I started to analyse the fieldnotes retrospectively that I felt I was following the gentamycin form through time as well as space. My method for analysis was to look through my fieldnotes and use post-it notes to indicate where I had recorded information relating to gentamycin forms. I transferred these onto the PDFs of the notebooks as comments, so that I could search the notebooks. I also went through the transcripts to find references to the gentamycin form. I related this information to diagrams and photographs. This early experiment helped me to conceptualise networks in the data. It must be noted at this point that the 'actor' in 'follow the actor' is isolated as a discrete entity, which seems incongruent with ANT. However, my approach was to navigate my data and to become sensitised to connections and associations, and the actor was a way of starting this process.

I continued with the 'follow the actor' approach for Cohort 2. Here, I used the sticker as the actor. I started to incorporate the photographs more, and to use the photographs to help me to navigate around the data. For example, the sticker would start out as a page of printed colour stickers which needed to be cut into individual stickers by a guillotine. Following these practices helped me to attune to associations and forces as the stickers were being made. I found that I started to use different types of diagrams and collages to help to find connections and associations. The metaphor of networks was helpful and helped me to draw out insights from my fieldwork. There were some parts of my analysis using networks where I concentrated more on the power and effects through associations. Using an actor as a starting point helped me to sensitise to relations rather than focusing on individual entities. I did not consider these approaches to be mutually exclusive: rather, I either identified an actor first to map the network, or I had effects as a starting point.

I made decisions relating to the anecdotes: some 'won', whereas others were excluded. These choices were political, in that they changed the way the chapter reads, and what is included and what is not. This chapter was therefore performed into being and shaped by practice: David was never hiding in the marble, his shape came from an assemblage of stone, implements and artists. In the same way, my research is not an innate 'thing' that I am representing, faithfully, through my writing. My writing is a thing in and of itself, shaping the reality that my research has become. It is neither right nor wrong, it just is, because there is no truth to measure it against. The focus of interest for this study is how the students were part of relational learning, and creating realities of SLISPs. The key points drew out insights from the anecdotes in the analysis and how these were described through the lens of the ANT dimensions of networks, symmetry, and multiple worlds.

Symmetry and multiple worlds

As I moved on with my analysis, I realised that other ANT concepts could help to describe alternative insights from the data. I drew on the concepts of symmetry and multiple worlds. I produced collages for cohorts one and two using photographs I had taken and annotated. I also constructed what might be termed 'narrative pathways'; these were similar to concept maps used in qualitative inquiry (Butler-Kisber and Poldma, 2011). Images and pictures can be problematic as these tend to assume a representation of the data and can sometimes reinforce boundaries around objects; my intention was for the visual diagrams to be creative rather than reductive (De Freitas, 2012). However, Decuypere and Simons (2016, p. 378) describe figures as 'descriptive objects in their own right' and as a way to highlight relations. The diagrams and images drew attention to the relations between entities and the assemblages of heterogeneous materials that gathered in different practices. In this research, I turned to images as way of analysing the data rather than trying to represent patterns. In addition to the assembling images, I developed a technique to challenge the boundaries around objects. By using the 'remove background' function on PowerPoint as mentioned earlier, and trying out different ways of cropping the photographs, I found I could isolate certain parts of the picture through the programme (an algorithm, I presume, that was based on light and contrast). The resulting images were of parts of bodies, bits of paper, scraps of waste, parts of tables, laptops and others that were hybrids. For example, one image was of some hands and a sheet of paper. This helped me to attune to hybrids and provided a way for me to represent connections and associations without separating out specific 'parts'. In other words, I could maintain the complexity and inter-relatedness without arbitrarily reducing by coding and categorisation as would have been the case in other approaches. For me, this was a contrast to theoretical approaches found in health which consider materiality as separate from the human and compartmentalised; approaches that list and lump together objects and people without considering how they are connected in practice. Because ANT draws out relationality, having a visualisation of hybrids such as paper-table-laptop or hands-form-sticker made it easier to avoid these reductions (Fenwick and Edwards, 2012).

Exploring SLISPs

This chapter has set out the ontological position of an empirical ANT approach, and how this shaped the research design from fieldwork to analysis. The ways in which I used the three ANT concepts of networks, symmetry, and multiple worlds to guide the analysis are explained in the next chapter. Looking at networks enabled me to identify specific areas and stories that I could trace through my data. The difficulty with networks was where to 'cut' the network (i.e. where to decide to stop). Symmetry offered yet another area of focus, drawing to attention some of the specific elements within a network, and the interactions and effects. Looking at the fieldwork as multiple worlds provided new insights that were not necessarily distinct from networks, but offered a different facet.

References

Adams, C. and Thompson, T.L. (2016). *Researching a posthuman world: Interviews with digital objects*. London: Palgrave Macmillan.

Ahn, S., Rimpiläinen, S., Theodorsson, A., Fenwick, T. and Dahlgren, M.A. (2015). Learning in technology-enhanced medical simulation: Locations and knowings. *Professions and Professionalism*, 5(3).

Angrosino, M. (2007). *Doing ethnographic and observational research*. Los Angeles: Sage.

Angrosino, M. and Rosenberg, J. (2011). Observations on observation. In: N.K. Denzin and Y.S. Lincoln, eds., *The Sage handbook of qualitative research*. 4th ed. London: Sage, pp. 467–478.

Anzul, M., Ely, M., Freidman, T., Garner, D. and McCormack-Steinmetz, A. (1991). *Doing qualitative research: Circles within circles*. London: Routledge.

Barad, K. (2007). *Meeting the universe halfway: Quantum physics and the entanglement of matter and meaning*. Durham: Duke University Press.

Bleakley, A. (2012). The proof is in the pudding: Putting actor-network-theory to work in medical education. *Medical Teacher*, 34(6), pp. 462–467.

Bleakley, A. (2014). *Patient-centred medicine in transition: The heart of the matter*. Vol. 3. Heidelberg: Springer Science & Business Media.

Bleakley, A., Bligh, J. and Browne, J. (2011). *Medical education for the future: Identity, power and location*. Heidelberg: Springer Science & Business Media.

Bruni, A. (2005). Shadowing software and clinical records: On the ethnography of non-humans and heterogeneous contexts. *Organization*, 12(3), pp. 357–378.

Butler-Kisber, L. and Poldma, T. (2011). The power of visual approaches in qualitative inquiry: The use of collage making and concept mapping in experiential research. *Journal of Research Practice*, 6(2), pp. 1–16.

Callon, M. (1984). Some elements of a sociology of translation: Domestication of the scallops and the fishermen of St Brieuc Bay. *The Sociological Review*, 32 (suppl 1), pp. 196–233.

Crang, M. (2003). Telling materials. In: M. Pryke, G. Rose and S. Whatmore, eds., *Using social theory: Thinking through research*. London: Sage, pp. 127–162.

De Freitas, E. (2012). The classroom as rhizome: New strategies for diagramming knotted interactions. *Qualitative Inquiry*, 18(7), pp. 557–570.

Decuypere, M. and Simons, M. (2016). Relational thinking in education: Topology, socio-material studies, and figures. *Pedagogy, Culture & Society*, 24(3), pp. 371–386.

Denzin, N.K. and Lincoln, Y.S. eds. (2005). *The Sage handbook of qualitative research*. 3rd ed. Thousand Oaks, CA: Sage.

Edwards, R., Biesta, G. and Thorpe, M. (2009). *Rethinking contexts for learning and teaching*. Abingdon: Routledge.

Engeström, Y. (2001). Expansive learning at work: Toward an activity theoretical reconceptualization. *Journal of Education and Work*, 14(1), pp. 133–156.

Fairclough, N. (2003). *Analysing discourse: Textual analysis for social research*. London: Routledge.

Fenwick, T. (2009). Making to measure? Reconsidering assessment in professional continuing education. *Studies in Continuing Education*, 31(3), pp. 229–244.

Fenwick, T. (2014). Knowledge circulations in inter-para/professional practice: A sociomaterial enquiry. *Journal of Vocational Education & Training*, 66(3), pp. 264–280.

Fenwick, T. and Edwards, R. (2010). *Actor-network theory in education*. London: Routledge.

Fenwick, T. and Edwards, R. eds. (2012). *Researching education through actor-network theory*. Chichester: John Wiley & Sons.

Fenwick, T., Edwards, R. and Sawchuk, P. (2011). *Emerging approaches to educational research: Tracing the socio-material*. Abingdon: Routledge.

Fenwick, T. and Landri, P. (2012). Materialities, textures and pedagogies: Socio-material assemblages in education. *Pedagogy, Culture & Society*, 20(1), pp. 1–7.

Fenwick, T. and Nimmo, G.R. (2015). Making visible what matters: Sociomaterial approaches for research and practice in healthcare education. In: J. Cleland and S.J. Durning, eds., *Researching medical education*. Chichester: John Wiley & Sons, pp. 67–80.

Flyvbjerg, B. (2011). Case study. In: N.K. Denzin and Y.S. Lincoln, eds., *The Sage handbook of qualitative research*. 4th ed. London: Sage, pp. 301–316.

Fox, S. (1990). Becoming an ethnomethodology user: Learning a perspective in the field. In: R. Burgess, ed., *Studies in qualitative methodology: Reflections on field experience*. London: Jai Press, pp. 1–23.

Gehm, S., Husemann, P. and von Wilcke, K. eds. (2015). *Knowledge in motion: Perspectives of artistic and scientific research in dance*. Bielefeld: Transcript Verlag.

Greenhalgh, T., Annandale, E., Ashcroft, R., Barlow, J., Black, N., Bleakley, A., Boaden, R., Braithwaite, J., Britten, N. and Carnevale, F. (2016). An open letter to the BMJ editors on qualitative research. *BMJ*, 352(i563).

Hammersley, M. (1993). *Social research: Philosophy, politics and practice*. London: Sage.

Harris, M. (1976). History and significance of the emic/etic distinction. *Annual Review of Anthropology*, 5(1), pp. 329–350.

Hassard, J., Kelemen, M. and Cox, J.W. (2012). *Disorganization theory: Explorations in alternative organizational analysis*. London: Routledge.

Kanger, L. (2017). Mapping 'the ANT multiple': A comparative, critical and reflexive analysis. *Journal for the Theory of Social Behaviour*, early view online. DOI: 10.1111/jtsb.12147.

Kincheloe, J.L., McLaren, P. and Steinberg, S.R. (2011). Critical pedagogy and qualitative research. In: N.K. Denzin and Y.S. Lincoln, eds., *The Sage handbook of qualitative research*. 4th ed. London: Sage, pp. 163–177.

Landri, P. (2012). A return to practice: Practice-based studies of education. In: P. Hager, A. Lee and A. Reich, eds., *Practice, learning and change: Practice-theory perspectives on professional learning*. Dordrecht: Springer, pp. 85–100.

Latour, B. (1987). *Science in action: How to follow scientists and engineers through society*. Cambridge, MA: Harvard University Press.

Latour, B. (1999a). On recalling ANT. In: J. Law and J. Hassard, eds., *Actor network theory and after*. Oxford: Blackwell Publishing, pp. 15–25.

Latour, B. (1999b). *Pandora's hope: Essays on the reality of science studies*. Cambridge, MA: Harvard University Press.

Latour, B. (2005). *Reassembling the social: An introduction to actor-network-theory*. Oxford: Oxford University Press.

Latour, B. and Porter, C. (1996). *Aramis, or, the love of technology*. Cambridge, MA: Harvard University Press.

Latour, B. and Woolgar, S. (2013). *Laboratory life: The construction of scientific facts*. Princeton, NJ: Princeton University Press.

Law, J. (2004). *After method: Mess in social science research*. London: Routledge.

Law, J. (2006). Traduction/trahison: Notes on ANT. *Convergencia, UAEM, Mexico* (42), pp. 32–57.

Law, J. and Hassard, J. eds. (1999). *Actor network theory and after*. Oxford: Blackwell Publishing.

Law, J. and Singleton, V. (2000). *This is not an object*. Lancaster: Centre for Science Studies, Lancaster University. Available at: http://www.comp.lancs.ac.uk/sociology/papers/Law-Singleton-This-is-Not-an-Object.pdf. Last accessed on 15th November 2017.

Law, J. and Singleton, V. (2003). Allegory and its others. In: D. Nicolini, S. Gherardi and D. Yanow, eds., *Knowing in organizations: A practice-based approach*. Armonk, NY: M.E. Sharpe, pp. 225–254.

Lincoln, Y.S., Lynham, S.A. and Guba, E.G. (2011). Paradigmatic controversies, contradictions, and emerging confluences, revisited. In: N.K. Denzin and Y.S. Lincoln, eds., *The Sage handbook of qualitative research.* 4th ed. London: Sage, pp. 97–128.

Martin, A.D. and Kamberelis, G. (2013). Mapping not tracing: Qualitative educational research with political teeth. *International Journal of Qualitative Studies in Education*, 26(6), pp. 668–679.

McLean, C. and Hassard, J. (2004). Symmetrical absence/symmetrical absurdity: Critical notes on the production of actor-network accounts. *Journal of Management Studies*, 41(3), pp. 493–519.

Mitchell, B. (2020). Student-Led Improvement Science Projects: A praxiographic, actor-network theory study, *Studies in Continuing Education*, 42(1), 133–146. DOI: 10.1080/015 8037X.2019.1577234 (Open access www.tandfonline.com/doi/full/10.1080/0158037X. 2019.1577234).

Mol, A. (1998). Ontological politics. A word and some questions. *The Sociological Review*, 46, pp. 74–89.

Mol, A. (2002). *The body multiple: Ontology in medical practice.* Durham: Duke University Press.

Mol, A. (2010). Actor-network theory: Sensitive terms and enduring tensions. *Kölner Zeitschrift Für Soziologie Und Sozialpsychologie.Sonderheft*, 50, pp. 253–269.

Nespor, J. (2014). *Knowledge in motion: Space, time and curriculum in undergraduate physics and management.* Abingdon: Routledge.

Pring, R. and Thomas, G. (2004). *Evidence-based practice in education.* Maidenhead: McGraw-Hill International.

Prosser, J. (2011). Visual methodology: Toward a more seeing research. In: N.K. Denzin and Y.S. Lincoln, eds., *The Sage handbook of qualitative research.* 4th ed. London: Sage, pp. 479–496.

Punch, S. (2012). Hidden struggles of fieldwork: Exploring the role and use of field diaries. *Emotion, Space and Society*, 5(2), pp. 86–93.

Ragin, C.C. and Becker, H.S. eds. (1992). *What is a case? Exploring the foundations of social inquiry.* Cambridge: Cambridge University Press.

Silverman, D. (2000). Analyzing talk and text. In: N.K. Denzin and Y.S. Lincoln, eds., *The Sage handbook of qualitative research.* 2nd ed. Thousand Oaks, CA: Sage, pp. 821–834.

Sørensen, E. (2009). *The materiality of learning: Technology and knowledge in educational practice.* Cambridge: Cambridge University Press.

Stake, R.E. (2013). *Multiple case study analysis.* New York: The Guilford Press.

Star, S.L. (1990). Power, technology and the phenomenology of conventions: On being allergic to onions. *The Sociological Review*, 38 (suppl 1), pp. 26–56.

Zukas, M. and Kilminster, S. (2014). The doctor and the blue form: Learning professional responsibility. In: T. Fenwick and M. Nerland, eds., *Reconceptualising professional learning: Sociomaterial knowledges, practices and responsibilities.* Abingdon: Routledge, pp. 38–51.

Chapter 5

ANT in the field

This chapter focuses on empirical research exploring SLISPs in a hospital setting. Three ANT dimensions, discussed in previous chapters (networks, symmetry, multiple worlds) are used to frame the research. These three dimensions are used to explore research in the field, concentrating on two cohorts: the first cohort as the improvement science project to investigate antimicrobial prescribing, led by a medical student; and the second cohort led by one medical student and two pharmacy students looking to improve insulin prescribing process using a temporary sticker. The cohorts correspond to the two case studies, and specific 'anecdotes' are drawn from these. Through the idea of network, learning is described as disruption that occurs as networks collide, picking up, and extending Nespor's Knowledge in Motion. The cases are developed to describe how symmetry can help researchers to acknowledge situations as relational, which assists in the refocusing on practice and away from human agency. Finally, the notion of multiple worlds from Law and Mol are followed, describing how these coexist or compete in workplace situations. Extracts from the fieldwork are used to demonstrate how insights were drawn.

Cohort 1: The antibiotic story

In this cohort, the medical student was piecing together the 'antibiotic story' of patients on two different wards, with the aim of improving antibiotic prescribing. The aim of the project (SLISP), for the medical student, was to implement an 'improvement' to the process of antimicrobial prescribing through engaging with improvement science methodology. Some of the changes were intended to be temporary in order to test the 'improvement'; once tested, more permanent changes would be implemented. In network terms, the final improvement would become permanent, or stable, where the improvement is enacted and integrated into work practices. However, this requires existing networks to become destabilised, which is disruptive to the assemblage of people and materials that have come together to repeatedly perform the practice. My observations traced how the project allowed the student to recognise existing networks of practice, introduce new networks, and identified where connections and associations were pliable enough to accommodate changes. The student was clearly invested in the endeavour: they spoke passionately and knowledgeably about antimicrobial stewardship and the need to raise consciousness to staff about the use of antibiotics in the context of antimicrobial resistance. The student spoke about how procedures could be improved by placing more of an emphasis on finishing the course of antibiotic medication at the right time, rather than prolonging treatment; about how intravenous antibiotics were sometimes continued despite changes to the patients' health and their ability to swallow oral antibiotics; about the rapid transfer of junior doctors to different wards, and the power dynamics of prescribing and reviewing medications. To the student, the project was a valuable contribution to improving patient safety. The student's job was to first piece together current practices of antimicrobial prescribing on different wards. My job, as an ANT researcher, was to observe and notice how materialities assembled into networks as the project was carried out.

On the hospital ward, information about antibiotics was distributed throughout the medical records such as the prescription chart, medical forms and patient history, in different files and in different rooms. I use the word 'information' with caution, as it implies some form of human agency involved in the processing and interpretation of inscriptions, and in the case of my ANT-guided research, I am trying to avoid such assumptions. I observed how some information the student sought was recorded on the patient notes held together on clipboards outside the patients' rooms or at the end of their beds'; in marker pen on notice boards; in clipboards kept on trolleys; in the huge, cumbersome patient history files with multi-coloured forms in a manila, cardboard file, precariously bound with thick, elastic bands. As I followed the student, I noticed the intricate choreographies that took place on the wards as humans and non-human materials assembled. I saw how the long, criss-crossing corridors led to doors that were locked or pushed open, guiding footfalls past a row of patient rooms or beds. I saw the dexterous manipulation of clipboards and paper as inscriptions controlling the patient's wellbeing were squinted at, copied, transferred and interpreted. I saw the quiet collaboration of trolleys, limbs, paper, and medications come together in opportunistic spaces.

The antibiotic story network: learning as disruption

As an outsider researcher with no knowledge of practices on hospital wards, the action, spaces, and materialities I first observed made little sense. I followed the medical student as they carried out their project, and the student explained some of the processes as we walked around the wards. Developing an ANT sensibility, I was conscious of the human-centeredness of this endeavour, and so I chose to 'follow the actor', the actor being a gentamycin form. Gentamycin is an antibiotic that is commonly administered before surgical procedures as a prophylactic. The dosage and timings need to be carefully calculated for each patient, based on individual measurements such as weight, and therefore a medical form has been devised solely for the prescription and administration of this particular antibiotic. Having the gentamycin form as an entry point was helpful to start the analysis by attuning to the relations and associations between different actants on the ward, rather than relying solely on the students' explanations, which foregrounded their own sense of what was important to know rather than allowing me to observe connections as they arose.

Referring to the questions pertaining to networks, the analysis of the 'antibiotic story' highlighted the importance of understanding how existing networks overlap with ones that are just forming. The SLISP, originally considered as being something contained, bounded, and newly introduced, is now re-presented through tracing the anecdote as a network in its own right, forming connections with other, existing networks. One of the insights from this part of the analysis is that medical forms, including the gentamycin form, are not objects that can be isolated from practice or from the patient, because the information they carry is contingent to practice. Berg and Goorman (1999) describe how information is extrapolated and moved around, sometimes without considering the contingent nature of the measurements. The student described how patient information is distributed throughout different networks, through roles, purpose, and materially:

> [I]t would make it a lot easier if all of this stuff was in one place. But again, because they have quite a lot of documents, and they all mean different things about, maybe different conditions, or whatever. I think it's easier for them to have everything separate, but when you're focusing on one thing, that involves bits and pieces from different bits, you kind of wish there was one thing . . . But again it depends for that ward where their priorities are . . . So yes, it's difficult when there are so many different things in different places! And stories that go back. Because every time the doctors speak to the patient, I'm sure it's probably the same for nurses as well, they need to document it in the notes. So they will say, I spoke to the patient about X, Y, or Z, or spoke with the relatives. So you end up with lots of pages of this big story. And I'm sure when someone goes back to see the patient they don't read every single page. They probably just skim through it and miss a few things; which, they have to document for legal reasons and stuff like that as well. But it does start to get a bit messy and you don't know what's going to be where

The SLISP network brought with it improvement science methods, including PDSA (plan, do, study, act) cycles, balancing measures, and run charts to name but a few. The 'antibiotic story' anecdote is a new network that formed associations and connections as the SLISP was introduced to existing networks. The aim of the SLISP was to ensure the new network becomes stable. My study did not go beyond the initial stages of the project, so it is beyond the scope of this study to comment on whether the improvement was taken up and stabilised as a network. The anecdote demonstrates how the SLISP forms a temporary network for the duration of the project, and that the practices of improvement science are then deleted. The notion of deleting practices comes from Law (2004), and refers to the way that repeated performances of practice become more refined, resulting in a sleeker process which brackets some of the complexity. Learning is manifest in associations and connections between the new network and existing practices. However, it must be stated that networks are in flux and require constant work to maintain stability. Nespor describes networks as 'fluid and contested definitions of identities and alliances that are simultaneously frameworks of power' (Nespor, 2014, p. 9).

It might be said that the student's research was de-centring the human by placing antibiotics at the centre; however, from an ANT perspective, there are a number of issues with this. First, that anything has to be at the 'centre' at all. Massey (2005) problematises spatial metaphors as a historical predilection towards cartography and physical space. The idea of a 'centre' could be described in ANT terms as an asymmetrical topography, that is, a privileging of physical space that does not necessarily exist in conceptual space. Second, there is a conceptual tension in ANT with universalism and essentialism. By putting forward the idea of 'patient–centred care' there is the idea of a universal 'patient'. This is further problematised by the notion of 'person-centred care'; calling someone a 'patient' highlights their medicalised self, one that requires treatment and is placed in a medical institution. Proponents of 'person-centred care' argue that the patient is a transient state rather than an identity, and that 'patient-centred care' does not take into consideration social and family issues that might contribute to health outside the medical world. However, both terms draw from a universalist and essentialist notion of the human as discrete and isolated. ANT, on the other hand, draws from ideas of association, and reinforces the idea that nothing exits in the same way in different places because of these associations (Latour, 2005). The idea of a patient might allude to the physical embodiment of a medicalised self, but it also acknowledges the relationship to medicine, policy, professionalism, the hospital, prescription forms, and so on. The combinations and relations form patient networks and the patient can be considered as distributed.

Materialities and symmetry in antibiotic prescribing

Having an entry point into the SLISP network through 'following the actor', in this case the gentamycin form, was helpful to start the analysis by helping me to attune to the relations and associations between different actants on the ward. I constructed narrative pathway diagrams (e.g. Figure 5.1) of some of the actants to assist with identifying relations and forces between actants and started the process of attuning to networks. I went on to explore the materiality of the medical documents further to draw out 'spaces or blanks' (Fenwick,

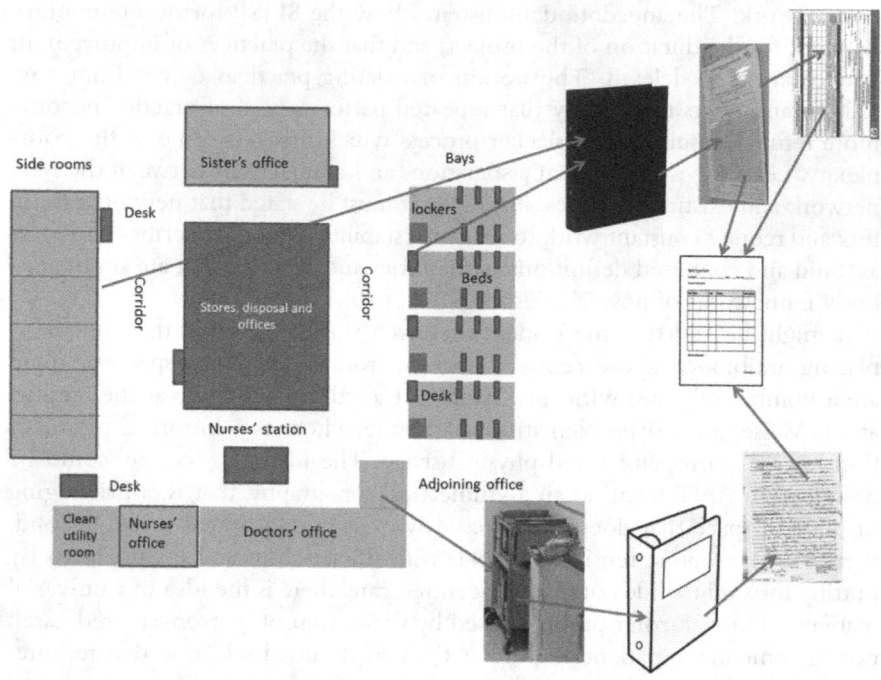

Figure 5.1 Narrative pathway

2011, p. 98) that might otherwise be overlooked, by turning my attention to the ANT dimension of symmetry. I started this by attending to the physical properties of the gentamycin form or chart.

The gentamycin chart has a red bar across the top and a sticky strip on the back. The protocol, as explained by the student, is to stick the form into a prescription chart in the correct fashion so that the red bar protrudes, making it prominent. The prescription chart is a folded A4 booklet made of stiff paper, and is used to record all the medications for the patient. The information on the gentamycin form is also written into the prescription chart so that staff can see what medications the patient has been prescribed, how long the medications have been administered, and when the medication needs to be reviewed. A member of staff explained to me in an interview about the significance of the sticky strip: in the past, the form had been inserted with other documents and had, on occasion, got lost. The absence of the form, when the patient arrived in surgery, led to a 'double dosing' of gentamycin, which can result in acute kidney infection. The materiality is a particularly significant part of this practice, with the sticky strip as a measure to ensure the patient's records were kept together. However, I observed several instances of the gentamycin form where the sticky strip either was not used, or where an old version or colour photocopy was used, suggesting that the new format had not been connected stably into the network.

The format of the gentamycin chart affected the SLISP, as it required physical manipulation to read, and then further effort to interpret the figures written on the sheet. The student could not collect everything in one place and had to become familiar with the layout of the ward, where the paperwork was kept, who was using it, and when. Piecing together the 'antibiotic story' required walking around the ward and finding the relevant folders and files. The behaviour of the student and other staff on the ward was affected by material assemblages. For example, at one point, a nurse had to wait for the student to finish with a file, and on another occasion, the nurse accidentally dropped a clipboard, dislodging the attached papers. The stationery that was used to contain medical forms on the ward invited different forms of practice: the double clipboards hung on the dado rails outside patient rooms. The physical shapes of the clipboards were not conducive to being moved around or stacked together, which regulated practice by keeping the clipboards on the dado rails next to patient rooms. The ring binders were more portable and more easily left in different places; however, there were trolleys, which allowed for ring binders to be kept together rather than distributed haphazardly throughout the ward. I recorded in my field notes:

> In front of each room a double clipboard hangs on the wall at waist height. [Student] checks the [prescription chart] from one of these, seated on a small wheeled table and chair . . . Some clipboards are fiddly, papers could fall out . . . Some notes on [prescription chart] are difficult to interpret . . . Gentamycin chart: stuck onto drug chart with sellotape.

In a later observation:

> Boards with lots of sheets, difficult to manoeuvre. One fell off when we tried to put it back on the dado rail.

The above quotes describe the assemblages of forms that are physically held together on clipboards (Figure 5.1), or stuck together with the sticky strip or sellotape. The physical manipulation of the clipboards to extract the gentamycin form is also combined with the complexity of reading the notes on the forms. This illustrates some of the effects (such as double dosing) of the configuration of the forms and the significance of ring binders and clipboards to reinforce the connections between forms. From the above examples it is shown that paperwork is frequently manipulated, inscribed upon, inspected, and moved.

The photograph to the left in Figure 5.2 depicts one of the double clipboards with a prescription chart and other medical forms. On the right is a trolley with ring binders. These trolleys can be moved around the ward; ring binders

Figure 5.2 Material configurations

can be taken out and put in other places. Because a range of staff use the pre-scription chart, the student found it was sometimes missing from the patient notes. Being handled by so many people, and so frequently, translates to mate-rial wear and tear of the document. When the prescription chart is new and blank, it appears a sturdy document. It is made of thin card rather than paper, and is a gatefold design with eight sides for recording prescriptions. It is printed in colour (light blue, dark blue, and red). In many cases the prescription chart will be put into a ring binder, so there are holes punched through the form on the left-hand side. The filled-in forms can get scuffed, and sometimes the holes wear through. A filled-in chart can be bewildering, with numbers, letters, and symbols in myriad boxes. In some cases, liquid stains are also evident. A single patient may have more than one prescription chart associated with them. Old prescription charts are supposed to be scored through. Handling the prescription chart can be problematic: the document opens out into a long document of four A4-size sheets. For the students, this means finding places to lean, finding places to rest folders on.

For the SLISP, the student walked up and down the corridors in the wards to obtain the relevant ring binders and checked these against the patient notes on the double clipboards. Getting to the relevant sheet involved physical manoeuvring, and there was a risk of dropping paperwork. Other staff were also looking for the files and ring binders:

> On the table is a patient file. [The student] leans on file on table to write; nurse comes out of the room and takes out a pen, pauses; . . . and she says 'Oh, it's OK, I'll wait for you'.

The interaction described in the extract above illustrates how staff manipulate the same materials, spaces, tables, and files. The nurse in this extract is part of a material assemblage, waiting with a pen to join the table, ring binder, and medical notes.

Throughout the student's data collection for the SLISP, ring binders and patient history notes were being moved around on the ward on a trolley for other staff to use, or placed on the nurse's station so that the staff member had a space to lean on whilst writing. The movement of the files and having multiple people trying to access the same piece of paper at once made for a complicated process for the student to collect the information needed for the SLISP. The student talked about the intricacies of collecting information from different physical places, and how this was confusing:

> I can tell the percentages are inappropriate just by using [this] chart. But it also means now that I also need to look at the blood results to see the white cell count. Which, in some cases it's in the notes, the patient's notes, in other cases they'll have a folder with blood results. I've not quite worked out, in [Ward], everyone seems to be in the Blood Results folders. But in surgery so far there's been some in notes and some in the folder, and I haven't quite worked out when they're putting them in the folders and when they're putting them in the blood folders. I don't know if that's maybe just a mistake . . . because they just popped it in the notes when they shouldn't have.

This is a significant realisation for the student, identifying the different physical sources and then also querying whether the forms are in the right places.

Piecing together the 'antibiotic story' from different sources required a lot of walking around the ward. As well as different forms, the forms were kept in different files and the files were moved around the ward. Patient history files were kept in the doctor's office; these are the large, manila, cardboard files that are thick and held together with an elastic band. Current patient notes relating to a particular ward were kept in ring binders, labelled with the room in which the patient was located; this is the folder that the student refers to in the above quote. Ward staff, including doctors and nurses, frequently moved these folders around the ward, sometimes leaving them on the nurse's station or on tables outside rooms. The Blood Results folder, mentioned in the example above, is another folder, kept at the nurse's station. The clipboards hung on a dado rail outside each room, and these were usually not moved around the ward. The configuration of the folders and forms required the student to physically move around the ward to collect information for the SLISP.

Another complication of manoeuvring materials was the student's own equipment:

> [Student] looked up drug on phone, [prescription chart] in hand . . . Clipboard under arm, pen in mouth. Then puts phone back in pocket, puts [prescription chart] back, writes with pen.

It was interesting to notice how the physical manipulation of the clipboards was also problematic for experienced staff:

> Nurse puts clipboard back and it slips, clatters to the floor. [Student] picks it up, the papers have come out. Nurse turns around and jokes 'Every time!' and laughs. Puts board back but it won't stay. Replaces it on floor.

This quote illuminates the intersection of the different worlds of the nurse and the student, through signposting to different practices. In the quote, the nurse is taking the forms off the clipboard to find out about the patient and to see whether there are medications to administer, whereas the student is looking across forms to piece together the 'antibiotic story' to inform the SLISP. These differences move our attention from the materials themselves and onto the spaces that open up to the different sets of practices. The professional identities of the student and the nurse form as effects, as connections are made to different networks of practice.

The material configuration and position of materials required the student to perform physical practices that would not have been taught in a classroom or a simulated ward, even though these are practices central to the work of a junior doctor. Another exclusion in the SLISP was the patient: in one ward, the patients were situated in side rooms and had become dispersed onto paper rather than the flesh-and-blood body in the bed. The student was performing patient care without coming into contact with the patient's body. As this example unfolded, there was a shift in the metaphors from networks to assem-blages. By focusing on the configuration of materials and the forces these produce, there is less emphasis on the relational and more on space. This is similar to Sørensen's (2009) findings that the network metaphor does not 'fit' all scenarios. The implications for learning in this section, therefore, begin to diverge from the relational, networked metaphor. Learning emerges from more spatial analogies, for example, how the materials are distributed on the ward. Distribution (Mol, 2002) allows learning and knowledge to become associated with spatial metaphors. The distribution of learning and knowledge is not only through space but through assemblages of human and non-human entities. The concept of symmetry therefore provides a way to think of learning and knowl-edge as distributed through 'things': 'In education, textual objects proliferate in such things as curriculum documents, maps, educational journals, parent news-letters, student record systems, exams, text books, competency lists, newspaper editorials, training software and test instruments' (Fenwick and Edwards, 2010, p. 8). In this example, textual objects such as the gentamycin form and the pre-scription form distributed knowledge, which was further carried through other objects such as ring binders and clipboards, and connected through points of translation.

The materialities pointed towards different worlds of practice, a metaphor developed in the next section.

The multiple worlds of 'duration': more than one and less than many

The student encountered ambiguity and difference when attempting to record a seemingly straightforward piece of medical information. The information related to the duration of time that a medication (in this case, an antibiotic) had been prescribed for. The requirements of the protocol are that the prescriber records when the medication is to be administered and for how long. However, the prescriber might not be working with that particular prescription to the end of its course, so decisions regarding whether to continue the medication, stop or change, are sometimes made by another clinician. A variety of roles are connected to this recording: doctors, registrars, consultants, nurses, and phar-macists. As mentioned at the end of the last chapter, different roles perform different practices that might include the same objects. In the case of recording duration, different members of staff use the same paperwork but for different purposes, signposting to different worlds of practice. As outlined during one of the interviews:

> [O]nce something's prescribed, it takes an active input to stop it from being prescribed. So if you don't do anything, it will just carry on. And the nurs-ing staff will keep doing it. So it takes an active action to go and say, actu-ally this has been on for a week, what are we doing about that? Can we

stop that? Can we change that? But if you don't have anybody necessarily querying that, if you don't do anything it will just stay on there and carry on. So it requires input to do that.

The student devised a form to collect background information for the SLISP, with a straightforward form with one 'yes/no' box, relating to the question of whether or not the duration of the use of the medication had been recorded. This seemingly simple binary unfolded to reveal subtle nuances: duration could be recorded in different ways, from recording the start date to the number of days the medication had been taken to date and so on. The process of ticking the box led to oscillating forces, tensions, and 'strain' of ambivalence (Fenwick and Edwards, 2010) as the recording of 'duration' revealed a multiplicity through different practices.

Boxes for recording 'duration' are indicated on the prescription chart. However, on visiting the ward, the student found that information regarding duration could not be collected as anticipated. I recorded this difficulty in my fieldnotes (below). This marks the first stage of exploring ambiguity, both for the researcher and the student.

> Some notes on the [prescription charts] are difficult to interpret – lots of different [Anti-Microbials] with different durations . . . Only current duration from sheets – not sure at this stage what needs to be recorded . . . 24/9 date format confusing in duration box (usually as 1/7 days)

At first, the idea of 'duration' was referred to by the student as a singularity, categorised in the same way as the type of antibiotic used. But the action of going into the ward with the intention of ticking a box then became a complex undertaking. The above quote is one example of when the student encountered ambiguity in recording duration. The standard format is [day] 1 of 7, recorded as 1/7. However, in the example cited, the numeric could be a date 24/9 (24th September) or a duration recorded as the ninth day of 24. On another occasion during the fieldwork, a nurse described how a small, yellow sticker was being used on the prescription chart to mark when that particular medication was required to be reviewed. The nurse presented the process as a way of changing the culture, process, and authority of recording prescribed medicines. The nurse presented duration as a process whereby the date for reviewing the medication is the most critical, and that nurses should have the authority to enable them to prompt the review to take place. However, when the yellow sticker was mentioned in a later meeting, a consultant was less than enthusiastic, highlighting some of the more nuanced decision making that sometimes took place.

For doctors, the prescribing is the start of the process, but the duration is something that continues over time, through shift handovers and staff rotations. The duration is decided at the start, regarding when to start the treatment and how long this should continue for. However, the decision might be changed if the patient is not responding as anticipated. Making the decision to stop or continue a medication sometimes requires extra work through testing the patients' levels, and perhaps a decision on switching from intravenous to oral or vice versa; it also requires an indication on the handover note to justify stopping a medication. These extracts illustrate the complexity that unfolds as the student attempts to record a simple 'yes or no' on their form, indicating if the duration has been recorded in line with protocol. This was further illustrated in a meeting the student had with their supervisors:

> Student: Yes well, I found so far that . . . because [consultant] was saying that so far she's told them all these indicators so they're now all aware that they're supposed to document duration. But I think there's been a mix-up somewhere, because they're all documenting duration 'so far' instead of 'total duration'. I double checked with the pharmacist and she said it's definitely how long they're going to give it for, not what day they're on. So I was on a ward round today and they were, 'Oh so that's day 7', so I was like . . . I don't really know whether to say something . . . now, or (laughter) it might be something that they tend to do as well . . . they would say, 'Oh yes, this is day 5', and then they're supposed to go on and say, 'For 7 days' . . . I don't know . . . I didn't want to say, 'Oh, don't write that', just in case that's something that they also write . . .
>
> Supervisor: Well you'd want them to write, 'day 5 of 7', wouldn't you? Just so it's clear!
>
> Student: So, all the ones that haven't documented the duration have actually documented 'so far' durations. So they've been scored as 'no', but . . . I think they think they have. So I'm going to go speak to [consultant].
>
> Supervisor: I think I would make a note of that when you see it . . . so if the answer's 'no' then it's because there's nothing, when what they've actually recorded is how long the person's actually been on it.

In this quote, the supervisor appears to make a clear decision as to what could be regarded as compliance with protocol when recording duration: 'day 5 of 7'. However, the student goes on to say that there are 'so far' documented durations; not in the correct format, but with the correct information. It is then agreed that non-compliance is where nothing is recorded as opposed to a 'so far' recording which is accurate but not compliant with protocol. It is important to note that, as well as the prescription chart, the student looked at other paperwork, such as the handover notes, to investigate why duration was recorded as 'so far' instead of being compliant with the protocol. This presented an interesting rift between adhering to protocol by recording duration as 'day 5 of 7' and the reluctance to exercise professional judgement by stopping a medication – possibly because the decision was made by a different doctor before handover, or possibly because of the additional work that is required to switch from intravenous to oral medication, or obtaining test results to stop a medication.

As noted in the interview earlier in this section:

> [O]nce something's prescribed, it takes an active input to stop it from being prescribed . . . if you don't have anybody necessarily querying that, if you don't do anything it will just stay on there and carry on.

There was also the example of the nurse describing how the yellow sticker enables nurses to have the authority to prompt a review, thereby strengthening protocol, and how the consultant was dismissive of this, suggesting that these might not be used properly. These examples illustrate the different processes involved in recording duration across roles, handovers, and staff rotation. Rather than dismiss these as different perspectives on the same thing, or as a deviance from protocol that can be corrected, it might be more fruitful to explore the different practices and enactments of duration that might be considered as multiple worlds.

The practices of prescription, administering, and review created different enactments of duration that were incommensurable, yet operated side by side. Differences were regulated through translation (in practice) and rationalisation (in discourse with supervisors). The practices are 'more than one but less than many' (Law and Hassard, 1999; Mol, 2002; Strathern, 2005) as they 'hang together' to perform duration but cannot be collapsed into a singularity. Partial connections (Strathern, 2005) refer to the inclusion of one entity within another and vice versa, but where the entities cannot be collapsed into a singularity (Law, 2004). This provides a way of thinking beyond binaries of 'one' or 'many'. The 'yes/no' tick box on the data collection form was changed by expanding the meaning of duration to accommodate different practices; this could be imagined as the SLISP challenging the 'yes/no' binary and accepting ambiguity as part of practice. This illustrates the tensions between the requirement of improvement science to be precise and exact, and the messiness and ambiguity of practice. The pursuit of the term duration allowed for an examination of detail into the enactment of prescribing practices, and how this translated into the SLISP for Cohort 1.

To help me, as a researcher, to attune to multiple worlds from my observations, I manipulated images from the photographs I took (Figure 5.3). The 'remove background' function on PowerPoint allows images to be created with boundaries around objects stuck together, rather than isolating discrete objects, which helped to envisage hybrids to 'rearrange humans and things to allow for new forms of technology, knowledge, presence and learning to emerge' (Sørensen, 2009, p. 13). The contingent nature of medical information has been explored in other studies (Berg and Goorman, 1999). Studies of specific forms, such as the Blue Form (Zukas and Kilminster, 2014) and the Integrated Care Pathway (Allen, 2013), have demonstrated how social practices cannot be

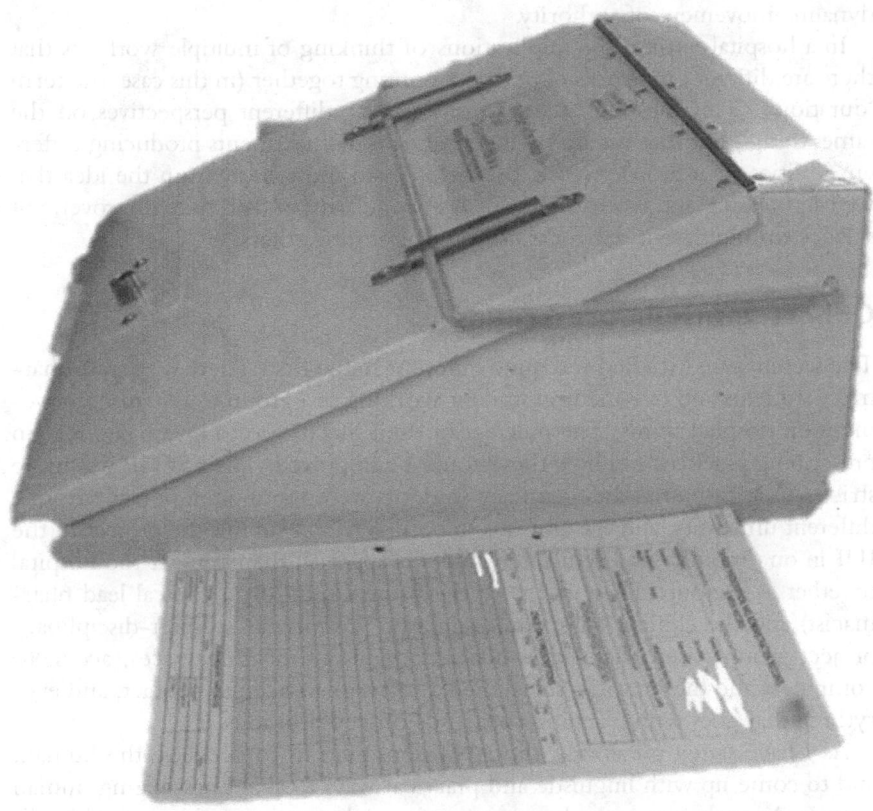

Figure 5.3 Hybrid picture

explicated from recording and translating medical information. This example has introduced an alternative reading of this phenomenon by describing how social and material practices are enacted in multiple worlds where medical information is entangled in practice. Learning was enacted in this scenario from the differences and multiplicity of recording duration, leading to a different version of the form with an explanation rather than a yes/no tick-box. The decisions made by doctors were translated onto forms and into boxes, but there were differences in the way information was recorded. Knowledge moved around, from the paperwork on the ward, to the consultant and the supervisors, and enacted in practice. However, prescription practices were subject to stronger forces that were not 'held' but circulated. Junior staff deferred to senior staff (Foundation Year doctors and pharmacists to registrars, for example). Staff rotation and availability also played a part; the absence of the surgeon on the ward (because they were in surgery) or the time of day also added to the dynamic movement of authority.

In a hospital setting, the implications of thinking of multiple worlds is that there are different networks of practices coming together (in this case, the term 'duration'). This means that we are not taking different perspectives on the same 'thing', but that we are paying attention to enactments producing different realities. In a broader sense, this helps us to move away from the idea that we can measure and evaluate SLISPs as a singularity, and abstract improvement science from different networks, implanting it into others.

Cohort 2: Insulin prescribing

The second case I studied was quite different to the first. There were two pharmacy students and one medical student working as a group to test an improvement on hospital wards. The purpose of their SLISP was to investigate insulin prescribing practices and how these could be improved. Their SLISP was more strictly time-bound as the pharmacy students were visiting temporarily from a different university, and the aim was to complete and submit the project to the IHI in one month. As a result, the students spent all their time at the hospital together as a group. They met with the project sponsor (a clinical lead pharmacist) and the clinical skills team regularly. Working as an inter-disciplinary project group raised challenges such as organising meeting spaces, access to computers and the internet, social media software to keep in contact, and everything that goes with reaching consensus on key decisions.

As I have stated previously, the ANT sensibility is to decentre the human, and to come up with linguistic and practical ways to avoid privileging human agency. As such, the preceding paragraph might seem at odds with this. To address this disparity, I would like to expand on the notions of 'medical' and 'pharmacy' student and how this might be described in the sense of human/ non-human relations. In the last section I described the problems with universality and essentialism in person- and patient- centred care, concluding that local networks ascribe meaning to people and objects through their associations and connections. The networks in which the students were enrolled included a range of weak and strong connections with materials such as equipment, paperwork, spaces, disciplines, procedures, and so on. In Chapter 1, I introduced The Locker, and how networks in which this acted produced effects of belonging and security. I also drew out associations between the locker and electronic software systems; this illustrates the positionality of humans and non-humans, and how they enact networks by coming together. The effects produced by the network are sometimes attributed, asymmetrically, to humans or non-humans on the basis of underlying assumptions. ANT enables for a more symmetrical analysis by noticing effects rather than attribution of cause to specific actants.

In research accounts there is often more of a connection between humans and emotions, with softer, ephemeral, and intangible effects attributed to human action. Objects are considered passive, inanimate, present, material, isolated, detached, discrete, and so on. I am not claiming here that objects have the capacity to feel or emote; that would be anthropomorphising (Johnson, 1988). However, an ANT reading would position feelings and emotions as network effects, generated by the interaction of humans and non-humans. Think, for example, of the frustration you feel when a file is overwritten on your PC, or when internet connection cannot be established when you are waiting for an important email. It is not the intention of your laptop to cause you upset, but that does not prevent you from imagining so, and reacting as though this was the case. The post-human aspect of ANT, expressed through symmetry, is usually either glossed over or played out ad-absurdum (McLean and Hassard, 2004). It is important to remember, as Latour describes, ANT is not about tracing the root cause of an action back to human intention. It is about flattening out practices that are operated and orchestrated through relational materiality. In the case of SLISPs, it is not necessary to draw a distinction between the number of students involved, rather to consider the wider networks this may bring together, the strength of these connections, and the effects produced.

The SLISP in Case 2 investigated insulin recording practices and how improvements might be made by prompting more specific information to be recorded on the Clerking Form, which is filled out when patients come onto the ward. In Case 1, the emphasis was on the prescription chart and gentamycin form. For readers unfamiliar in hospital procedures, this illustrates the amount of paperwork surrounding each patient, the different points and locations at which information is recorded. This might also highlight tensions with improvement practices. Staff need to negotiate myriad forms and paperwork to confirm patient information, and improvements necessarily disrupt these practices. Hospital wards are busy places, and although improvements are welcome, it is acknowledged that disruption should be kept at a minimum. If several improvements are being tested simultaneously, it could potentially add to the complexity of ward practices.

The network effects of the sticker

In Cohort 2, a temporary sticker, with boxes for additional information relating to insulin prescribing, was used to alter the clerking form and to prompt the person filling it out (usually a junior doctor). The students decided to make the sticker pink in colour as other medical forms relating to insulin were pink. The purpose of this for the SLISP was to test whether the introduction of the temporary change via the sticker would lead to more accurate recording of insulin for patients who are dependent on insulin, and ultimately lead to fewer incidences of hyperglycaemia. For the students of Cohort 2, the sticker became the focal point of their project. This example explores how, rather than focusing on the students as change agents, and alternative would be to explore the forces that emerge from the connections between entities and the effects these have such as learning, identity, behaviours, and so on. As outlined in an interview with student:

> It wouldn't be a sticker forever. The problem you have is that when you integrate stuff onto a form, it then blends into the background. And people don't necessarily fill it in. But it is . . . it's balancing: is the insulin a high enough risk medicine that you need a completely accurate prescription, with is it worth getting it to blend into the back of the paper.

In this quote, the sticker could be conceptualised as producing network effects. The quote suggests differing strengths of connection in the network; for example, a permanent change to the form might weaken the network effect by 'blending into the background'. This suggests that the effect of the sticker is a stronger force in an unstable network, whereas a permanent change to the form might be a weaker force in a more stable network.

During the first student cohort meeting, the clinical lead outlined the aims and planning for their project. As the project needed to be completed in a month, the clinical lead had already set up the project and gave the students a brief outline of how the project might continue from this. The students were instructed to complete a PDSA cycle for each stage of the project, as part of the rapid tests of change. The students were also required to complete other IHI Practicum documentation, such as a run chart, cause-and-effect model, and a final report at the end of their study. In a similar way to Cohort 1, in this study the IHI Practicum templates are conceptualised as a new network that would overlap and create connections with other networks. After the project, the network connections would either form a stable network, or, once the IHI Practicum is no longer part of the network, the new network might become unstable. The work to stabilise the new network involved the students consulting with staff members on what they thought of the sticker in order to produce a version that would be most relevant to their practice. Once an agreed version of the sticker was produced, the students needed to monitor the number of insulin-dependent patients and whether the sticker had been completed for these patients. One of the students explained the purpose of the sticker and some of the difficulties the group encountered:

> So we started off with a sticker that had already been sort of tested by another group and then we took it on version 3. And then we created like a form using Google Drive, where we knew what feedback questions we wanted to ask clinicians when we asked them to use it. But to begin with, we were trying to catch diabetic patients and get the clinician to actually use it for a diabetic patient. But we found out that, on that ward, there wasn't a high rate of diabetic patients, so we had to sort of adjust our method of testing. So we decided to use scenarios [patient simulation], where we'd come up with insulin regimes, and then we would test that

with the sticker instead. So we used the feedback form, got a clinician, and just sort of pretended to be a patient, got them to fill it out and then used the feedback form to sort of create a structure to what questions we were going to ask them. And what answers they gave us as well.

Not all the staff were accommodating to the students' requests for help and participation in the patient simulation, although many were very helpful and took time to work with the students. At this stage, it could be seen that the SLISP was forming its own networks that were interrupting existing networks on the ward. The students were attempting to destabilise the existing practices of medical reconciliation and create a more detailed recording system for insulin. The patient simulation enabled connections to begin forming during the project: the sticker destabilised the networks around the admissions form (for insulin-dependent patients) by presenting an alternative way of recording. It was possible that the sticker would be overlooked because of stable existing practices resisting the change, but the sticker (and its prominent pink colour that connected to insulin recording) and the students (through patient simulation) were participating in the improvement being 'performed into being' (Fenwick, 2011). Resistant forces not only included a lack of participation from the staff, but also authority and senior staff preventing participation:

> They said the doctors were not buying in to it, that they told them to come back at 6 – this sounds like they are being fobbed off . . . [the students] were saying that one of the [Foundation Year doctors] seemed keen to do the feedback, but another clinician (I think he is a registrar) stopped them from participating.

The extract from the fieldnotes illustrates that the lack of participation from some staff was creating destabilising forces in the SLISP network, in turn, stabilising the existing ones. The students persevered in their efforts to get the sticker integrated onto the form by continuing to speak to staff and ask for feedback. There was encouragement from other clinical staff regarding how to make the sticker more likely to stand out and to be noticed by staff, so these would get filled in, further supporting the medical student's idea of the sticker being more prominent. Discourses of selling, such as 'buy-in' can be seen as network effects that work against resistance. A stabilising effect on the network, the colour of the sticker, creates an association with the pink colour of forms relating to insulin. During an observation, one of the students notices the colour pink in amongst other paperwork, and immediately associates this with information pertaining to insulin:

> [The student] goes to look for a file for side room 2 as [they see] the pink form on the clip-board . . . Gets clip-board from the outside of the door . . . Goes to sliding scale on pink form . . . Goes back to file and pink

prescribing form . . . gets the big patient file and flicks through to one of the pink forms.

The students were hoping that the colour change would indicate the association to insulin and invite staff to complete the details. Changes to the sticker were documented by the students on electronic feedback forms that they created themselves, and then recorded on PDSA cycles. When the students agreed on changes to the sticker, the next task was to go to the pharmacy office to meet with the clinical lead and to print some stickers off. The task required a colour printer and a guillotine, which were situated in the pharmacy office. The pharmacy office is located on a lower level, down a very long corridor. There is a buzzer system on the office doors with two buzzers. During the observations we would sometimes have to wait ten minutes or more for the clinical lead to come to the door. The buzzer became an Obligatory Point of Passage (OPP) for the SLISP network, that is, a central assemblage 'through which all relations in the network must flow at some time' (Fenwick and Edwards, 2010, p. 18).

The sticker created small effects on the network whilst the students worked with clinical staff to form connections with the existing networks of practice, such as the association of pink with insulin recording forms. Connections were formed with willing staff, but resistance came from some junior doctors. The result was a network in flux, precariously held in place with a temporary sticker, the effects of which were strengthened by staff feedback and the patient simulation exercise. The students recorded changes to the sticker on PDSA cycles, and mapped existing practices on process diagrams. As the SLISP progressed, associations formed between the students and the IHI Practicum templates, becoming stronger as electronic formats of the templates, such as the fishbone diagram, were repeatedly returned to, and created links with electronic software (Google Drive, Slack, IHI Practicum) and hardware (PCs, Wi-Fi, electricity). Manual forms were excluded from the process, further reinforcing links with electronic practices. The IHI Practicum created forces that governed how the tests of change were carried out (e.g. through the PDSA cycles and the fishbone diagram) and how the SLISP was enacted. However, another network of practices formed around the physical production of the sticker, including the effects of the pharmacy office and its buzzer system as an Obligatory Passage Point (Callon, 1984). The connections created effects of learning for the students as new connections were made; in the 'formation of linkages with learning as an effect' (Zukas and Kilminster, 2012, p. 44). And in terms of network effects:

> knowledge is generated through the process and effects of these assemblages coming together . . . learning itself becomes enacted as a network effect.
> (Fenwick and Edwards, 2010, p. 4)

In other words, knowledge can only maintain its status within the network, can only exist in association with other entities and is held in place through associations (Nespor, 2014). The IHI has meaning for the students; the IHI network overlaps with the SLISP, which in turn overlaps with existing practices. The examples given described how these networks assembled, overlapped, and the enactments that held them together. In terms of what learning is being created for the students, being enrolled into the IHI Practicum network by undertaking the SLISP creates connections through the assemblage of materials such as the electronic templates; being on the ward creates connections with existing practices, such as the pink colour of the insulin forms and carrying out patient simulations with staff; and connecting these two networks to create an improvement that interrupts current working practices and requires ongoing work to maintain.

Symmetry and the sticker

In this anecdote, symmetry is a focus to highlight points in the data that might otherwise be overlooked. The well-known magic trick of sawing a woman in half is a good example of practices that are overlooked and made invisible. During the trick, a (usually) female assistant enters a box, lies down, and pokes her feet out at the end of the box so the audience can see she is lying down. The magician then produces a saw and proceeds to saw the assistant in half. The boxes are separated, then put back together. The glamorous assistant emerges whole and unharmed. The trick is that the audience assumes that the assistant is doing no work and is lying passively in the box, like an object. However, the assistant is actually contorting their body into the upper part of the box, whilst the feet at the end are actually false feet, which the assistant pushes out through holes at the end of the box. This illustrates how assumptions can render some practices invisible. When observing workplace practices, if it is assumed that only humans do work and objects are passive, then some actants will be overlooked. One solution would be attending to detail during observations; another would be noticing other sources, such as interviews, stories, and accounts that shine a light on practices that are invisible. The anecdotes in this chapter illustrate how the researcher could have 'missed a trick'.

Whereas the learning-as-transmission tale (Mulcahy, 2014) is traditionally measured through the retention of knowledge, situated learning requires a different approach. Sociocultural approaches to learning are focused on the collective, rather than the individual; materials are considered, but the human is still privileged with agency, and is the subject of assessment. ANT considers the sociomaterial as symmetrical, focusing on the actions of both human and nonhuman with equal interest. Conceptualising networks allows the researcher to attune to connections and associations from which learning emerges as an effect. Symmetry enables the researcher to notice the forces and effects of relations by considering the workplace practice as 'flat': that is, not imposing a hierarchy such as valuing human activity above all else. Thus, the taken-for-granted practices that are rendered invisible by privileging human action can be considered. In this chapter, the sticker and other parts of the network, human and non-human, challenge the position of the student as a change agent, and instead agency is considered as dynamic, not fixed, and as flows and forces between elements rather than properties of these; as McLean and Hassard (2004) argue, ANT focuses on effects and outcomes rather than 'things'.

A criticism of ANT is that powerful actors tend to be scrutinised more closely, which detracts from mundane detail and everyday practices that are necessary to explore in order to account for that which is taken for granted or overlooked. In this example, the sticker might be one such powerful actor. However, the sticker, in this example, is considered as an entry point to the data to explore some of the practices around the sticker rather than the sticker itself. There is much to be said about how materials invite/exclude or regulate participation in practices. For example, a human-centred account of the sticker would be: 'the students took the sticker paper to the pharmacy office and printed the formatted sticker on a colour printer. The students then cut the stickers with a guillotine to produce separate stickers. The students then peeled off the paper backing to stick the stickers onto the appropriate place on the medical reconciliation form'. This highlights the difference between sociocultural approaches and socio-material approaches: the students are placed at the centre and are the only ones acting in the situation. In a socio-material account, the language needs to reflect relations and forces rather than sources of agency.

The secret drawer

An example of practices that have been overlooked is the 'secret drawer'; this term was used informally by the students, but reported on in the IHI Practicum report as 'a different location'. This refers to something that happened outside the observations, but which had a powerful effect on the SLISP. The sticker was being stuck onto the medical reconciliation part of the admissions form to add boxes to the medical reconciliation, for the purpose of recording more detailed information about insulin. In order to get the sticker filled in, the form needed to be placed in a prominent position; there was a risk that forms without stickers would be used instead, and then the insulin form would not be completed. The students were advised by the nursing staff to place the stickered forms at reception. However, the students found out that the doctors on night shift kept a stash of forms that were unstickered, in a 'secret drawer' as the reception desk was closed at night:

> [The medical student] fed back on the night shift . . . the [ward] Reception desk is shut down on the nightshift, so the FYs have a stash of forms in the doctors' room. The team were not aware of this, so now they can change the procedure to accommodate this.

Extract from shared electronic notes:

[10:19 AM] feedback meeting: We're struggling with the sticker implementation, is this a bigger issue with regards to insulin prescribing.
[10:20]

secret doctor stashes of paperwork have been identified
[10:21]

having the form in the paperwork incorporated doesn't = paperwork being
completed

The 'secret drawer' is an example of 'missing a trick'; although the students and
staff were aware that there was a different shift operating at night, they were not
familiar with the different practices. In this case it was an insight made by the
medical student from talking informally to a junior doctor who had been on
the nightshift. The medical student made the connections to the paperwork not
being completed due to the different location of the forms. The familiarity at
that stage with practices, and the configuration of materials, allowed the group
to understand the significance of the secret drawer. What ANT and symmetry
bring is the attention to detail leading to this: the inclusion of a sentence in the
IHI Practicum report does not reflect the surrounding practices and the effect
of the students in realising that this was significant. These are situations where
learning effects occur from making practices visible that would otherwise go
unnoticed and unrecorded.

How the locker became a force to be reckoned with

Another actant that created unexpectedly strong effects in the network was the
locker. The pharmacy students were studying at a university almost 70 miles
away from the hospital, so had to commute and were reliant on trains and
buses. To get to the hospital from the train station required a bus ride of 20
minutes or more, so, however long the train took, the bus would add time to
the journey. This meant that the pharmacy students found it difficult to arrive
at the hospital early or to stay late. Their commute was at least two hours each
way and they were both reliant on connections. The medical student was living near the hospital and had a car, so was better placed to come in early or
stay late.

The medical student was based at the hospital and was allocated a locker
in the locker room for medical students. They shared their locker with the
pharmacy students and myself, although it was not big enough for everyone's
belongings. To do so, the medical student shared the door code with us and

left the key in a pair of shoes which were left on top of the locker, so that the other students could get access when required. At first, the pharmacy students and myself put valuable items in the locker. However, because the medical student also needed access, they would sometimes hold on to the key. The group would post messages on Slack to say where the key was, who had it and who needed it next. The other students and I used the locker room to store backpacks and coats but took equipment (iPads and valuables) with us. It was against the code of conduct to walk around the wards with big bags and coats, so we all tried to keep what we had with us to a minimum. We were all reliant on the medical student to use the locker, as this was their allocated space. Some tensions arose in the group. At the start, the medical student set up the online groups and was highly conversant and skilled on using the applications. However, the other two students did not have the same experience and were unsure about using these. The medical student persisted with the idea and the other students learned how to use the applications; these became the main means of communication between the group members. The electronic format necessitated electronic equipment – but this required safe storage; the locker was not big enough or easily accessible, despite efforts by the team to co-ordinate where the key was being kept. In a different type of research, the tensions might have been interpreted as a clash of personalities or explained as individual behaviours working in a group. However, the analysis through ANT would be as a network of humans and non-humans and the resulting effects.

The expectations of a doctor are different to those of a pharmacist and these are reflected in the training they are given and how they are treated by staff. The medical student would be expected to take charge of intense situations and to possess qualities to be relied on to step in. Being a student in the hospital, it was an expectation that they would be able to organise work spaces for the other students and show them around. However, analysis using networks has identified the locker to be a powerful actant in this network, creating forces and effects that influenced the way the group went about their project. The ambiguity over access to the locker affected what the pharmacy students left there. Although the medical student was as accommodating as possible, there was still only one key that all three students required access to, and limited space. One of the pharmacy students did not bring in a laptop, partly due to this arrangement, and consequently all electronic work was done using the medical student's laptop. The reliance on electronic formats was reinforced throughout the project through online forums and sharing sites. Returning to the questions at the start of this chapter, the assemblage of materials required to produce the electronic rather than manual format of the IHI forms ultimately shaped the practice of the SLISP and affected the learning that emerged.

To analyse the agency of the locker in more detail, I followed a suggestion by Latour under the pseudonym Johnson (1988), of drawing up a table where one column lists all the effort that would go into a task if a certain object (in this case, the locker) was not there, thus demonstrating 'tiny efforts balance out mighty weights' (Johnson, 1988, p. 299). In the case of the locker, if there were no lockers, students would have to carry things around with them, and make sure that these things did not impede work whilst on the wards; they would also be more likely to lose things or have things stolen. This exercise illuminates the status of the locker and other things within practices. The students from Cohort 2 occupied different learning spaces such as the main concourse, teaching rooms, the locker room, the library, and the pharmacy offices. This movement made it more important to have somewhere to store things and not to carry them about. Analysis using a network view demonstrated a stable network of electronic devices and online tools which facilitated a way of working to accommodate commuting distances and out-of-hours working. However, this configuration produced a specific reading of the SLISP that might have looked very different in different circumstances. Drawing from the notion of symmetry, the agency ascribed to human activity can be reconfigured to attune to the forces exerted by materials within the network.

Hospital spaces: assembling multiple realities

Traditional concepts of professional learning concentrate on skills acquisition, personal attributes, and the growth of knowledge, which can be measured and evaluated (Mulcahy, 2014). But what does learning look like as a socio-material assemblage? This section highlighted how learning is relational, with the focus on 'associations or connections or relations through which matter and meaning, object and subject co-emerge' (Mulcahy, 2014, p. 56). A truly symmetrical account might come from the point of view of the object itself (for literary examples of this, see Parker, 2016; Bush, 2019). However, I would argue, following Mulcahy (1999, p. 81), that, 'I came to understand that the tale I was telling of my network was complicit with the tale it was telling of itself'. In other words, the descriptive account is entangled with the fieldwork, and not a layer that can be analytically separated. In my research, I drew out details in fieldnotes and accounts that included materials and described how these shaped practice, such as working in electronic format. The anecdotes cited this chapter show how decisions can be made in the workplace that perform a particular type of reality. As Mol (1998) argues, if practices shape reality, then it follows that multiple practices lead to multiple realities. Choices and decisions are made as to which reality to perform into being, which is referred to as an act of ontological politics. The decisions made regarding which realities to perform need to address: what is at stake? In the case of SLISPs, an 'improvement' is an enactment of practices where the improvement might be evident in some practices but not others.

Early on in Cohort 2's project, the clinical lead took the students around the 'surgical floor', which can be visualised as a number of wards in a row, joined together by interconnecting doors. I found it difficult to record fieldnotes by hand during the visit, as we were walking around quickly and sanitising hands at every sink we passed. I therefore recorded reflective notes immediately after the event:

> [clinical lead] took us through the wards, through linking corridors and back doors. This gave the effect of the 'Surgical Floor', rather than segmented as distinctive wards, a mass of rooms and beds that all linked together. By negotiating around the surgical wards it gave a labyrinthine feel which contrasted with my previous experience with [Cohort 1]. It was disorientating and dizzying, our senses were assailed as we followed [clinical lead]'s quick steps, stopping at each alcohol hand-wash dispenser, ducking out of the way of staff, squeezing past beds and trolleys.

This extract illustrates how the same physical space had been enacted differently at different times. The concept of the ward presents segments that are separated by doors, a main entrance, and the position of the nurse's station as a form of reception desk. The notion of the same space as part of the surgical floor opens up the space, allows for flow through the corridors. Mol (2002, p. 55) describes the enactment of knowledge in hospital spaces:

> [T]he building isn't divided into wings with doors that never get opened. The different forms of knowledge aren't divided into paradigms that are closed off from one another. It is one of the great miracles of hospital life: there are different atherosclerosis in the hospital but despite the differences between them they are connected.

The worlds of the ward and the floor hang together through use of the doors: the wards keep the doors shut, the floor opens them. The doors are not locked and it is not prohibited to move through them, it is working practices that affect how the doors are used. Other factors are the trolleys, which are mobile; the beds on wheels; and the corridors. At each entrance/exit there is hand-sanitising gel, which invites the practice of movement by providing a way of sterilising the hands at each point. If the gel was not there, staff could not sterilise their hands, which would not be considered safe. Therefore, the position of the gel grants permission for traversing the floor through the back doors instead of the main entrance. The doors were not locked at the back of the ward, enabling staff to pass through from one ward to the other, as the clinical lead (a pharmacist) demonstrated. However, staff rotation and procedures also impact on how these realities 'hang together': the junior doctors ascribed to a ward for a period of time, and the nurses employed by the ward, would not have cause to enact the floor in the same way.

Staff rotation for junior doctors was usually two months on one ward, whereas the pharmacists were placed for a longer period of time covering multiple wards on the same floor. Nurses are employed by the ward. The difference in practices influenced the way different health professionals conceptualise the ward and the floor. For example, when I arrived on a ward, I sought permission from the Senior Charge Nurse as this person was considered to be in charge of the ward, even though they were not necessarily the most senior staff member present on the ward. From the observations with Cohort 1, explorations of different wards took place by entering and exiting through the main entrance, and no attempt was made to use back doors. The connection between different enactments of the clinical space and clinical roles was emphasised in an interview with a pharmacist:

> [W]e don't have enough pharmacists to have one pharmacist per ward, is the bottom line . . . we just don't have the resource to do that. So we spend some time on the ward, and we spend time on whichever other wards. Whereas the junior medical staff, so the FY1s and the FY2s, they are associated to one ward only . . . And the nursing staff obviously will work on the one ward all day as well. So they're there the whole time, for the whole shift and on that one ward. And then they come back the next day and they're on the same ward.

The above quote highlights the role differences between medics and pharmacists. This is significant for the students in Cohort 2, as they were an interdisciplinary team. In the case of the pharmacy students, the possibilities affect the space that they enact their practices within, challenging the concept of the ward and opening this out to a floor. These enactments relate to the professional practices of the students: although the medical student in Cohort 2 was more familiar with the ward, it was the pharmacist clinical lead who enacted the floor. In terms of Cohort 2's SLISP the implications were about how they themselves, as medical and pharmacy students, negotiated spaces between wards to conduct their project. The guided tour by the clinical lead highlighted differences in the enactment of space by different professional groups that might have been overlooked if the project had been limited to doctors and medical students. The differences challenge the conditions of possibility for both professional roles by presenting the option of walking through different corridors and doors between wards. Other studies have focused on the connections between learning and inter-professional practice. For example, Falk, Hopwood and Dahlgren (2017) drew from Schatzki's concepts of commonality, where practices are shared and have things in common, and orchestration, where practices are different but affect each other, to describe how knowledge was shared inter-professionally. In this story, inter-professional practice is explored through difference in the way that space was enacted by Cohort 2 as they carried out their SLISP.

Clinical spaces were integral to both cohorts. Being on the ward was an important part of the project for experiencing work in the hospital. The students' experience of the wards highlighted the feelings of discomfort experienced by the pharmacy students, and the familiarity of the medical students to the clinical environment. In addition to the enactment of clinical space as signposting to professional practices, this study explored the use of spaces beyond the wards as sites of learning for the SLISP. Ahn et al. (2015) presented learning spaces as socio-material arrangements that create conditions for learning. Whilst it must be acknowledged there may be other reasons for the enactment of wards and floors, for example political decisions to reduce staffing costs (Mendoza, 2015), it is interesting to note how the enactment of physical space affects practice and creates multiple worlds.

For a medical student, the conceptualisation of the ward as a discrete unit, or closed system, might limit the conditions of possibility. The patients move about between wards (with their associated paperwork), as do specialist staff such as pharmacists, physiotherapist, and nutritionists, which creates an ambivalence in spatial terms. However, the nurses and FYs have a dominant presence in wards, which could make their reality more explicit through discourses of the ward and enactment of ward practices. The consideration of physical space and who decides how the space is used, is an act of ontological politics. Conceptualising a 'floor' might broaden conditions of possibility. The concept of collateral realities (Law, 2009) reimagines how space can be enacted. There is an explicit function of some of the places in the hospital: the ward is where clinical work is enacted, and where patients and workers are situated. This version of reality is explicit; the ward layout presents the ward as a unit, the reality of which is reinforced by the nurses, FY doctors, patients, bays, doors, nurses' station, and so on. However, this reality can be reimagined by roles which function across wards, on the 'floor', such as pharmacists: this can be termed a 'collateral reality': 'realities that get done incidentally and along the way' (Law, 2009, p. 1). The collateral reality is performed rather than known, and shifts the focus from a singular reality to a multitude of practices which create different realities. The collateral realities of corridors, stairways, waiting rooms, rest areas, and locker rooms are also brought into being by assemblages that perform multiple realities. As a caveat, the intention of this research was to explore possibilities and observe multiple worlds as they exist in hospital practices. The ward/floor observation does not take into account historical occurrences where cost savings from staffing a 'floor' rather than a ward have led to understaffing in some cases (Mendoza, 2015).

Sørensen (2009) warns against the idea that a particular space is a domain or container for particular roles to be enacted. In Mol's (2002) study, for example, different enactments of atherosclerosis were evident in different places, but this does not mean that the place performed a version of atherosclerosis. The locker room was performed into a learning space by the students, as were corridors and waiting areas. Choices were made at throughout the project to use electronic forms and to work together as a group, which enacted a particular world of practice and identities for Cohort 2; however, different worlds may have been possible if the choices made had been different. The choices refer to ontological politics and conditions of possibility.

As discussed in earlier chapters, knowledge is commonly considered as acquisitional, and learning as a property, attribute, something that can grow, or increase in size. This is partly because of the language used and the biological and psychological models that have been associated with education for so long. The problem with this is that it limits the possibilities for educationalists. Conceptualising learning as a network effect helps to build an alternative language in medical education. The concept of multiple worlds extends this to challenge the conditions of possibility. If we follow a scientific path in research, we subscribe to an essentialist view. To extend this, we can say that our research views the object of our inquiry from different perspectives, to converge or 'triangulate'. ANT says the opposite. If we accept that, rather than perspectives of the same thing, we are studying different or multiple worlds, then the 'object of inquiry' becomes decentred; it becomes more than one and less than many. The physical space becomes different worlds that are enacted in different ways. It is either opened out or sectioned off. What pulls the world together are the practices that become unique to that space. What opens it up are the nomads that move across the floor at different timescales and through the unlocked doors.

Research summary

This chapter has described a piece of research to explore improvement science practices in a hospital setting through observing two SLISPs. The ANT principles of networks, symmetry, and multiple worlds were drawn on to produce insights about situated, socio-material learning. For cohort 1, the practices of a medical student piecing together the 'antibiotic story' was described as a network of interconnecting materials including the gentamycin form, trolleys, ring binders, roles, wards, and so on. This was developed into the idea of an assemblage, where the research focused on the symmetrical aspects of human and non-human materials being brought together and creating forces, which either helped or hindered the SLISP. The record of 'duration' signposted to multiple worlds of practice through uncertainty, ambiguity, and ambivalence. Cohort 2's SLISP followed a medical student and two pharmacy students as they explored improvements to insulin prescribing practices using a temporary sticker. Actor-networks emerged through completing electronic forms from the IHI Open School Practicum to record the improvement, and the development of the sticker itself. The effects of non-human actants, such as the locker, demonstrated how assemblages came together to enact the sticker. Enactments of learning spaces, such as the contrast of floor and ward, demonstrated new conditions of possibility to challenge existing practices and the politics behind realities that are performed into being and those that become collateral realities. The ANT dimensions of networks, symmetry, and multiple worlds are extended in the next chapter, where the empirical study explores the pedagogies of improvement science.

References

Ahn, S., Rimpiläinen, S., Theodorsson, A., Fenwick, T. and Dahlgren, M.A. (2015). Learning in technology-enhanced medical simulation: Locations and knowings. *Professions and Professionalism*, 5(3).

Allen, D. (2013). Understanding context for quality improvement: Artefacts, affordances and socio-material infrastructure. *Health*, 17(5), pp. 460–477.

Berg, M. and Goorman, E. (1999). The contextual nature of medical information. *International Journal of Medical Informatics*, 56(1), pp. 51–60.

Bush, T. (2019). *Cull*. London: Unbound.

Callon, M. (1984). Some elements of a sociology of translation: Domestication of the scallops and the fishermen of St Brieuc Bay. *The Sociological Review*, 32 (suppl 1), pp. 196–233.

Falk, A.L., Hopwood, N. and Dahlgren, M.A. (2017). Unfolding practices: A sociomaterial View of interprofessional collaboration in health care. *Professions and Professionalism*, 7(2).

Fenwick, T. (2011). Reading educational reform with actor network theory: Fluid spaces, otherings, and ambivalences. *Educational Philosophy and Theory*, 43 (suppl 1), pp. 114–134.

Fenwick, T. and Edwards, R. (2010). *Actor-network theory in education*. London: Routledge.

Johnson, J. (1988). Mixing humans and nonhumans together: The sociology of a door-closer. *Social Problems*, 35(3), pp. 298–310.

Latour, B. (2005). *Reassembling the social: An introduction to actor-network-theory*. Oxford: Oxford University Press.

Law, J. (2004). *After method: Mess in social science research*. London: Routledge.

Law, J. (2009). 'Collateral realities', version of 29th December 2009. Available at: www.heterogeneities.net/publications/Law2009CollateralRealities.pdf [Accessed 11 Nov. 2017].

Law, J. and Hassard, J. eds. (1999). *Actor network theory and after*. Oxford: Blackwell Publishing.

Massey. (2005). *For space*. London: Sage.

McLean, C. and Hassard, J. (2004). Symmetrical absence/symmetrical absurdity: Critical notes on the production of actor-network accounts. *Journal of Management Studies*, 41(3), pp. 493–519.

Mendoza, K.A. (2015). *Austerity: The demolition of the welfare state and the rise of the zombie economy*. Oxford: New Internationalist.

Mol, A. (1998) Ontological politics. A word and some questions. *The Sociological Review*, 46 (S), pp. 74–89.

Mol, A. (2002). *The body multiple: Ontology in medical practice*. Durham: Duke University Press.

Mulcahy, D. (1999). (actor-net) Working bodies and representations: Tales from a training field. *Science, Technology, & Human Values*, 24(1), pp. 80–104.

Mulcahy, D. (2014). Re-thinking teacher professional learning: More than a representational account. In: T. Fenwick and M. Nerland, eds., *Reconceptualising professional learning: Sociomaterial knowledges, practices and responsibilities*. Abingdon: Routledge, pp. 52–66.

Nespor, J. (2014). *Knowledge in motion: Space, time and curriculum in undergraduate physics and management*. Abingdon: Routledge.

Parker, H. (2016). *Anatomy of a soldier*. London: Faber and Faber.

Sørensen, E. (2009). *The materiality of learning: Technology and knowledge in educational practice*. Cambridge: Cambridge University Press.

Strathern, M. (2005). *Partial connections*. Walnut Creek, CA: Altamira Press.

Zukas, M. and Kilminster, S. (2014). The doctor and the blue form: Learning professional responsibility. In: T. Fenwick and M. Nerland, eds., *Reconceptualising professional learning: Sociomaterial knowledges, practices and responsibilities*. Abingdon: Routledge, pp. 38–51.

Zukas, M. and Kilminster, S. (2014). The doctor and the blue form: Learning professional responsibility. In: T. Fenwick and M. Nerland, eds., *Reconceptualising professional learning: Sociomaterial knowledges, practices and responsibilities*. Abingdon: Routledge, pp. 38–51.

Chapter 6

Pedagogies of improvement science

This chapter incorporates the cases with a focus on the pedagogies of improvement science, and the orientation within professional and practice learning. The ANT reading of improvement science can also be translated for other innovations and approaches. SLISPs are enacted differently in different situations, but the two commonalities are: improvement science methodology is used; and projects are led by students. Improvement science became an effect of both SLISP networks, but different in nature between the cohorts. The improvement science methodology and the different ways in which the two cohorts connect with it is explored in the first section. In the second section, student project leadership is explored, including how the projects were 'sold' to staff to form connections with existing networks.

Reflections about SLISPs

At the start of my project, I was introduced to the idea of improvement science, and connected with specialist groups. I read and discussed current literature in improvement science through these groups, in the context of quality improvement and implementation science. Later in my project I narrowed down my area of research to SLISPs. The Institute of Healthcare Improvement (IHI) and the IHI Practicum became a way of identifying what was 'in scope' for the SLISPs. However, because improvement science was in the early stages of being introduced to the NHS, there was an opportunity to explore it before a universal meaning was imposed. In healthcare there is a propensity to 'find a common language' to apply to evaluations and studies so they can be compared and synthesised. However, I realised the 'scope' of SLISPs varied depending on different student professions and quality improvement projects. For staff on the ward, SLISPs were an extension of an audit, for students they were part of their work experience. For some clinical staff, SLISPs were seen as an opportunity to implement improvements in a short period of time. For the students themselves, SLISPs enabled them to lead hands-on projects in the workplace. During my research, I observed the students working with a range of staff, from consultants and clinical leads to administrators and librarians. The practice of a SLISP was enmeshed with everyday practice and real-life scenarios.

Throughout my research and following the SLISPs for Cohorts 1 and 2, I became aware of differences and ambivalences in how the projects themselves were set up and presented. At the start of my research, I understood the SLISP as a bounded, short-term project that students could lead, and which drew from improvement science methodology through the IHI Practicum Open School. However, I realised that SLISPs took on different forms, with students conducting longer projects, working in groups or leading a project alone. I realised there were different enactments of the SLISP, relating to how the improvements were introduced, managed, led, and presented. In this section I explore the differences between the two SLISPs and go on to probe ambiguities in Cohort 2's SLISP. The purpose of this is to demonstrate the coexistence of the multiple enactments of SLISPs and the implications on learning. The question becomes: is consensus required as to what constitutes an improvement science project, or can different enactments coexist? And what is at stake if improvement science projects are standardised?

IHI Practicum network

This chapter explores the overlapping networks of the IHI Practicum and the effects this has on the SLISP. The practicum enacts knowledge in a particular way through a set of online teaching modules and templates for different stages in an improvement project. The IHI itself is an international body of experts who specialise in improvement in healthcare. IHI activities, chapters, contributors, are gathered on their website. A SLISP is organised around a set of paperwork and culminates in a project, which is submitted to the IHI website. During both projects, there were notable instances of powerful network effects that influenced the way the SLISPs were carried out. This section further explores how improvement science creates effects through the IHI and how the IHI, as an existing network, connects to networks of practices in the wards as the SLISPs are carried out.

The medical student from the first cohort had experience of the IHI practicum in previous projects, and was familiar with the paperwork. Their project did not involve the visible completion of this paperwork; instead, this became a 'mindset'. For example, the student found that the IHI templates for the PDSA cycle were not necessary to carry out a PDSA:

> Well, the PDSA cycles were really useful. And I find that you do it even though you're not aware sometimes of you doing it. Because you kind of get into that mindset of: OK, I'm going to do this and I've got to plan this, and then you go try it and go: right, what should I change? And then you change it; and then you're doing it without thinking about it. So, I will

definitely take that forward, but kind of make it more explicit when I'm doing a PDSA cycle, because I think it helps look at your kind of progress from where you started and what you've changed.

Cohort 2's precise following of IHI practicum required the group of one medical student and two pharmacy students to complete online forms and templates, which was explored in the previous chapter. Although an ANT reading with a focus on networks is useful for examining learning and knowledge through the IHI practicum, closer treatment with symmetry as the main focus is also helpful, as the practices are entangled with technology and software. Cohort 2 were using the IHI practicum documents for the first time. Theirs was a four-week project, ending with the submission of the SLISP onto the IHI website using all the indicated paperwork. The forms and templates were electronic, so the group opted to complete these online. This influenced the materialities of developing the project, as there was a perceived need for the group to work in spaces where they had access to electronic equipment. At one point, one of the supervisors overseeing the project sent an example of a 'cause and effect' or 'fishbone' diagram to the students via the Slack site, which the students had set up themselves.

The diagram was a simple, manual drawing, and was dismissed by the group because it was not the IHI template. This exclusion strengthened the group's reliance on electronic means for the SLISP. The electronic template brought its own set of problems that created network effects:

> As they put together the fishbone diagram, the only line left is under 'measurement', so they discuss what else they should have in that category. Formatting the fishbone diagram seems to take a lot of time and negotiation; the model is not easy to manipulate. They check through notes for amends to fishbone from feedback from meeting this morning.

As this quote demonstrates, the fishbone model was the driver for how the students presented information. The line under 'measurement' was referring to a physical line on the template. Each line represents a different concept, centred on the 'problem', in this case, hypoglycaemia. The template comes with six 'bones' to indicate a particular issue (e.g. measurement) with smaller 'bones' indicating details of that issue. The students had found that they had a blank line and felt they needed to fill it in. Rather than having the issues as the driving force, the diagram was the driver: as Law (1994, p. 12) points out, 'First, you need to draw a line between two classes of phenomena by distinguishing those that drive from those that are driven'. In this case, rather than deciding how many 'causes' and 'effects' needed to be recorded in relation to hypoglycaemia, the students took the number of bones on the template as the number of causes they needed to have, classing the diagram as a phenomenon that drove practice, rather than the students. The fishbone diagram could also be viewed as inviting practice (Fenwick, 2014); the blank 'bone' that the students felt compelled to fill in could be an example of blankness, which is used as a pedagogical device to prompt further thinking (Sørensen, 2009).

The IHI Practicum documents were accessed online, but there were opportunities for the students to work off-line. For example, the fishbone (cause-and-effect) template that was sent to the students through Slack was a different version to the IHI and seemed to invite the students to draw their own template and decide themselves how many 'bones' they would have. This demonstrates the strength of the electronic form, as the manual form was overlooked despite being more flexible; when the students came to complete the diagram, they went straight to the electronic template, and no-one mentioned the manual diagram. The electronic templates created strong network effects in Cohort 2's SLISP, both strengthening the connections to the IHI Practicum procedures, but also weakening connections with other possible ways of doing the project. The reliance on electronic forms also strengthened the connections with hardware (iPads, PCs), software (Google Drive, Slack) and other entities (Wi-Fi, electricity, connections, and points). The IHI Practicum, in Cohort 2, could be described as a 'network of prescription' (Fenwick and Edwards, 2010, p. 91) as this is what was promoted for the group members to adhere to. The manual diagram offered a 'network of negotiation', where other forms of diagram could have been included from outside the IHI, but this was not taken up.

Discourses of selling and resistance

Other network forces could be identified through discourses of selling and resistance. The clinical lead frequently spoke about 'creating will'; also the other mentors (academic leads) emphasised the need for developing skills in resilience and persuasion.

> [Training Lead] said other [SLISPs] students have had run-ins with the staff . . . understanding the culture . . . surgery is the hardest . . . depends on consultants, registrars, surgeons.

At the time, and in conjunction with other fieldwork experiences, the training lead mentioned in the above quote seemed to be making a case for the students to be more persuasive and resilient, and that having a 'run in' with staff was not unusual. This indicates the forces and effects holding existing networks together, and also the resistance to new networks.

For the student in Cohort 1, their previous experience of SLIPs gave them an introduction to existing practices and how a SLISP can be introduced to a ward:

> [N]ormally as a student you kind of go in and stand in the background, stay out of the way as much as possible and you didn't really want to annoy

anyone or kind of give people more work that they should. So it was interesting to go in and actually work as part of team. And you found that a
lot of people were quite enthusiastic about improvement. There was some
people that had been involved in projects their selves, so it was really good
just to kind of feel as part of that team.

This quote highlights what it is like for a medical student on a ward and the
expectations staff have of students. In terms of the SLISP, the student acknowledges the forces of staff on the ward: that they can 'get annoyed' or be enthusiastic, and that this is significant and can have an effect on the project. I had
observed staff annoyance and enthusiasm on the ward, but hearing the student
say that this had the potential to influence the project reinforced the strength of
selling or resistance as network effects.

Later on, the same student gave some specific examples of what had been
learned and could be applied for the next SLISP:

[I]t's always worth going on and speaking to everyone when you first go
onto a ward, just to find out, kind of what their role is. And even getting
their opinion on what they feel should be changed. Because one of the
things that I think I, not struggle with, but the kind of 'buy-in' to what
you're doing. So you'll always find that some people are like, yeah, this is
great. Like I really think this should go ahead and this is what we should
be doing. Whereas other people were kind of like, 'We've already got a
few things we need to do, that's another thing that I need to think about';
or: 'I'm so used to doing it this way, I don't want to change it'. So it's kind
of, you kind of need that communication. So, though, they feel that why
you're doing it is important, so that they're willing, so teamwork's really
important in that way, as well.

There were some notable situations with Cohort 2 where I was able to observe
staff behaviours towards the students and their project. This influenced the
mobilisation of knowledge around the network. In this first example, the pharmacy students experienced hostility from ward staff whilst they are collecting
data for their SLISP:

Coming back from ward, [student] said [they] felt uncomfortable doing
the data collection, more so than doing the feedback because people were
not as accommodating on the ward as they were on the last one. It was very
busy and people didn't seem to have time. The nurses were busy and didn't
seem to have time to help when [the student] asked where the notes were
kept . . . It seems a lot harder for the [pharmacy] students as they don't
know roles, timings etc., and the medical students do. Also, the [medical]
students are more likely to know and bump into people.

This excerpt also highlights the difficulties experienced by the pharmacy students in particular. In Cohort 2, there were many examples of the forces of behaviour and how these affected the projects at points of translation in the network. Their identities as medical and pharmacy students are not a given, but are enacted through network effects, and might be performed differently in other networks. What it means in practice to be a student in either of these disciplines is how the identity of the student is performed. For example, the medical student spoke confidently about being on a ward, negotiating the paperwork, and speaking with staff. In contrast, the pharmacy students spoke about feelings of discomfort, feeling overwhelmed, and 'chucked in at the deep end'.

I was conscious of existing networks of practice as the students entered the wards; human and non-human actants were organised according to ward practices. The forms, folders, electronic information, tables et cetera were accessed by several types of staff. There were codes of conduct relating to walking around the ward and acceptable clothing. The networks of staff roles, power dynamics, experiences, responsibilities for life and death decisions, policies, protocols, forms, recording procedures, extrapolating patient knowledge, other risks to health, economic pressures, technological change, cumbersome old records, test results, levels, and vital signs, these were the networks that the students were walking into. As a commentary to the previous sentence, it is with caution that lists are used in ANT: words and the names that are attributed to things may be the same length and contain similar letters, but what they describe are not similar. A good example of this is from (Borges, 1974) and the Celestial Emporium of Benevolent Knowledge, which comprises an incongruent taxonomy of animals with awkward juxtapositions and categories, including ones that belong to the emperor, mermaids, and those that look like flies from a distance. The piece describes the absurdity of arbitrarily grouping things together, and draws attention to what is included or excluded when it comes to lists.

Walking into an unfamiliar, busy workplace was daunting for the students, especially when encountering resistance from staff. The clinical lead for the project created counter-forces by encouraging the students to 'create will' with the staff, and offered to use their own authority to enforce the improvement. The training manager and supervisor also reinforced this idea by talking about resilience. The students expressed surprise at being pushed to continue interactions and to be more insistent, but as the project progressed, the students acted more confidently. The staff also gave encouragement and praise:

> I didn't ever anticipate that we'd have to be like, selling it . . . I thought we would just be recording what had been already implemented or something like that. So I didn't expect to have to go and seek out people to try . . . But I suppose that that's all, I suppose that this project's about. We've kind of just had a more front-line role than I thought we would have.

This quote highlights the implication from education of encouraging students to develop leadership skills, and relates back to traditional concepts of education as individualised and competency-based. However, an alternative reading could be: in order to mobilise knowledge, different parts of the network need to be performed and are stabilised around the IHI Practicum and SLISPs. To recall Mulcahy's (2014, p. 56; original emphasis) 'tale' of learning as: 'associations, or connections, or relations through which matter and meaning, object and subject, co-emerge', helps to describe how the effects of relations are important, and not just the attributes of the entities.

Stabilisation of SLISP networks

Cohorts 1 and 2 were at different stages in their SLISPs. The student from Cohort 1 had completed improvement science projects already, and was very familiar with the templates and the procedure. This experience formed a stable network of practices, and enabled them to take forward the improvement science methodologies as a 'mindset' rather than completing a set of templates; this implies that improvement science, in this case, had become mobilised. In other words, connections and translations took place on the projects the student was involved in, which created learning effects. Cohort 2 were new to improvement science projects, and were relying on the templates as a way of negotiating learning through the project. The network for Cohort 2 was forming, and still unstable. For both cohorts, the SLISP was performed into being. Cohort 2 completed an electronic Fishbone Diagram in favour of trying a manual one, further reinforcing the links with the electronic IHI templates, and forming network connections with electronic hardware and software and discourses of IHI. Discourses of selling and resilience became forces of persuasion and resistance in the SLISP networks for both cohorts. The roles of medical and pharmacy students illustrate the forces of behaviour at points of translation in the networks. Effects of fear and resilience emerged from the collision of existing and new networks, which is particularly strong for the pharmacy students who were new to the wards. The question: 'what gets left out?' draws attention to a notable exclusion: the patient. Although the patient is mentioned in accounts, the flesh and blood, embodied patient is not included. Although the students do not engage directly with patients during the project (with the exception of asking permission to look at notes if necessary), the patient is still present as a network effect through medical records. The patient's body could be viewed as a manifest absence, where the presence of the paperwork creates and exemplifies the absence of the body (Law, 2004).

Networks and learning in improvement science

For both cohorts, there was the tension of interrupting existing networks of ward practices with an 'improvement'. This 'improvement' formed a network in itself, starting with strong connections with the IHI Practicum, and forming partial connections with existing practices. As the projects progressed, the IHI network (which included the students as actants), disengaged. What stayed with the SLISP networks were connections and alliances that required continued performance and work in order to maintain an improvement. For Cohort 1, the improvement aim was a clearer sense of records relating to antibiotics which was achieved through building the antibiotic story. In Cohort 2, the sticker remained on the medical reconciliation forms on the wards, but once these ran out, the students would not be there to continue the improvement. The network effects of learning would necessarily change after the students completed the project, but the connections and alliances with the IHI Practicum meant that the students would be able to connect improvement science to other workplace practices in the future. This was the case with Cohort 1, where the templates were no longer performed into being in improvement projects, and were replaced with a 'mindset'.

Conceptualising networks can help the researcher to empirically record associations and relations, and to seek and see them more easily. Without ANT, the researcher might focus their attention on specific people or things, especially those that are more highly featured than others. The following sections take from two ANT concepts: symmetry and multiple worlds. These concepts attune to different parts of the research to produce alternative readings, and to address the 'spaces or blanks beyond networks' (Fenwick, 2011, p. 98).

The symmetry of online practices

Networks of practice have previously been described in this chapter in relation to the connections with improvement science methodology, particularly in relation to the IHI practicum paperwork. The IHI paperwork had strong effects for Cohort 2 and how they conducted their SLISP. Decisions were made at the start of the project relating to how the students engaged with the online resources. This section extends the practices of Cohort 2 and how symmetry, rather than a privileging or compartmentalisation of humans and non-humans, helps to draw out specific insights.

The students from Cohort 2 were required to submit an electronic report at the end of their four-week placement. They were working towards a collective project, but needed to submit the same report individually to the IHI Practicum in order to be individually accredited. At the start, the students needed to register their project and submit an IHI Charter, outlining what they intended to do. The final submission had to include PDSA cycles, a run chart, a process flow-diagram, a cause-and-effect (fishbone) diagram, and a final report. All the required templates were available electronically. The reliance on electronic forms meant that the practice of carrying out the SLISP was entangled in electronic equipment and practices. The configurations of equipment affected learning and the places where the SLISP was carried out by the students. For example, the students spent a lot of time in a meeting area where they could sit together with a laptop, teaching rooms, and the computer lab. In the computer lab, the students were able to sit in a row and all work on the same document at the same time using Google Docs. In the teaching room, the students could all see a screen and what was being written.

> Big screen so we can all see. [student] logs into BMJ project and adds [pharmacy student] as a member then [medical student] QI Insulin project.
> Call up Process Flow Template on BMJ. Moves table and chair so [medical student] can reach keyboard comfortably and look at screen. The keyboard is connected by a cable. Not wireless.
> They can add into the image using boxes, text & arrows. [medical student] explains the admissions procedures: minors, majors, paeds, resus.
> [pharmacy student] looks up the process model that [medical student] put up previously on [her/his] phone.
> While [pharmacy student] looks (discovers there is no service) [medical student] uses the drawing toolbar to see if shapes can be added. They can. So they use the shapes instead of words in the diagram to denote roles.

In this situation, the electronic equipment is setting the conditions of possibility, and this is also influencing practice by the movement of the table and chair; cables restrict the position of the keyboard, there is no service on the main PC. The medical student uses a phone to bring up the process model, and one of the pharmacy students uses the keyboard to bring this up on the screen. Practices are focused on what comes up on the screen. The drawing toolbar allows for shapes to be used in the diagram as a substitute for text.

As the two pharmacy students continue to complete a process diagram, the medical student introduces other equipment:

> [Medical student] uses flipchart to draw out what [s/he] thinks the process model should look like. [Pharmacy student] stands and points to shapes on the screen to say where [s/he] thinks things should go.

The two students stand and sit as they look at different parts of the process model on the screen. In this situation, the screen, keyboard, and flipchart create forces that shape where the students sit, stand and position themselves. In addition, the assemblage of materials that allows for the process model to be worked on (the computer equipment, internet, software, flipchart, pens, tables, and chairs) are located in a room (teaching room) in an area of the hospital away from the wards, but connected by corridors and doors. In spatial terms, the assemblage of materials and humans (students) occupy the same proximate space. In temporal terms: booking the room, walking to the room, setting up the equipment and spending time drawing the process chart using software, all impact on the learning practices around the SLISP. Another observation that could be made is on the process model itself and how this produces a carto-graphic representation of the process. As Law and Singleton (2003) discussed in their exploration of mapping trajectories, representation is not neutral, and necessarily makes epistemological and ontological assumptions. In the case of the SLISP, a final process map was agreed upon by the students, but this was constructed with negotiation and compromise, and shaped by an assemblage of materials.

The choice at the start of the project to complete the forms in electronic format shaped how the SLISP was carried out by organising learning spaces where PCs and internet connections were available. Working as a team on the electronic forms affected things such as: how the electronic equipment was used and by whom; who contributes to the online discussions; how documents are merged; and, how conflicting ideas are represented electronically. The electronic format created conditions of possibility through the materials, and this was illustrated through working in rooms where materials were available such as Wi-Fi, screens, keyboards, and cables. In the previous chapter, I relayed the story of the locker, 'How the locker became a force to be reckoned with'. The strength of the locker network can be understood from the previous description about Cohort 2's reliance on electronic equipment following their commitment to electronic forms from the IHI.

Multiple worlds of SLISPs

For Cohort 1, ambiguities were openly discussed and negotiated during supervisory meetings. The student leading the project had been part of other group SLISPs in the past, and was experienced on the wards. Cohort 2's SLISP was a bounded project that was submitted to the IHI at the end of the project, using the IHI electronic templates and procedures. The contrast of the two cohorts highlights how projects of a different nature gather under two aspects: projects that are led by students and utilise improvement science to implement a quality improvement. However, the degree to which the students lead the project also illustrated difference. The student from Cohort 1 decided on the improvement and made key decisions to shape the SLISP with minimal input from the supervisory team; Cohort 2 had an improvement allocated to them by the clinical lead, and met frequently with the clinical lead and the training manager to discuss key decisions. The use of improvement science also varied between the cohorts: Cohort 2 filled out the electronic templates from the IHI throughout their SLISP; Chris from Cohort 1 considered improvement science as a 'mindset'.

One of the key contacts in my research presented SLISPs in a way that held open controversies and ambiguities. This key contact referred more to quality improvement than improvement science, and referred to quality improvement as a particular group of people and a particular way of doing things. Their ideas of SLISPs relating to the IHI Practicum further opened out difference:

> I want them [students] to be more involved in research with the process of understanding theory and theory based interventions rather than, oh we thought this would be a nice way of doing things . . . versus, OK, let's see what's out there, let's see what could fit with this particular context. So at least, a little bit more systems thinking in that sense, throughout the process of research, rather than more fragmentary based on some rigid rules and regulations from IHI.

The contact's presentation of SLISPs was different to that of Cohort 2, whose project was centred on the IHI Practicum. However, Cohort 1 was more closely aligned with the above version, which could be due to having experience in doing previous SLISPs. The training lead also emphasised the ambiguity of SLISPs:

> [T]here are different ways to approach things, and there's not always a right or wrong way. There are good basic principles, but I think if you've got students who are first time doing this and trying to learn, you want to make sure that they are getting a clear message. And that they're clear on what they're doing. Because I think the overall process, as we see each time when we do this, is that the students go through a big journey. And very much, very unsettling for them because this isn't straightforward. And also their priorities and the way they plan things out, the timescales, do not always really fit within a clinical environment.

It could be said that improvement science was enacted between people and other elements. As Mol (2002) describes in the 'doing' of a medical diagnosis: 'two people are required. A doctor and a patient. The patient must worry and wonder about something and the doctor be willing and able to attend to it' (Mol, 2002, p. 23). Mol's argument is that the diagnosis is performed into being, rather than being an essential element waiting to be discovered. In a similar way, improvement science is enacted and performed as part of SLISPs. It might be said that two people are required to enact an improvement: clinical staff of the ward need to be convinced that this will improve practice, and the SLISP student has the time and commitment to attend to the improvement.

For Cohort 2, the enactment of the SLISP presented ambiguities through the PDSA cycles. Cohort 2 were sent links to the IHI Practicum, and had completed most of the modules prior to starting. The cohort attended a presentation by the training team to explain the rationale for improvement science and the project they would be undertaking. The students were told that their project was more about learning the processes of improvement science (like learning a new language) and working together as an interdisciplinary team. The IHI Practicum was introduced along with all the associated paperwork. The students were told what they needed to do within their four-week placement and how to submit the project at the end. The time-scale of Cohort 2's SLISP was a factor in the reliance on the IHI Practicum paperwork. The time-boundedness created a boundary for Cohort 2, where there were few resources to challenge ambiguities around their SLISP. Nonetheless, some ambiguities arose through the enactment of the project tools, most notably, what constituted a PDSA cycle. During their induction, the students were told:

> PDSA is most important; this could be talking to a staff member about a sticker: need to predict what you think the outcome will be. All need to be written up.

Later on, the students in Cohort 2 complete what they consider to be their first PDSA cycle. However, the clinical lead disagreed with their judgement:

> [Clinical Lead] disputed the first PDSA, this was more about engagement and buy-in. [Student] pointed out that [training lead] had a broader view on PDSA. [Clinical Lead] clarified that PDSA is about a test. Test is different from a task.

The exchange illustrates how improvement science is still open and contested through the enactment of the practices of SLISPs allow for negotiation and difference in relation to how the PDSA is carried out and what it is for. In the case of Cohort 1, PDSAs had become a 'mind-set' rather than a procedure:

> Well, the PDSA cycles were really useful. And I find that you do it even though you're not aware sometimes of you doing it. Because you kind of get into that mindset of: OK, I'm going to do this and I've got to plan this, and then you go try it and go: right, what should I change? And then you change it; and then you're doing it without thinking about it. So, I will definitely take that forward, but kind of make it more explicit when I'm doing a PDSA cycle, because I think it helps look at your kind of progress from where you started and what you've changed.

This quote shows how the PDSA has become part of practice, rather than a form to fill in. The discrepancy about PDSAs between clinical staff highlights their different practices: the clinical lead was more conversant with the operationalisation of PDSAs as part of improvement science, whereas the training lead was more concerned with the students from Cohort 2 learning to use the 'tools' of improvement science. In this case neither version 'wins', as the PDSAs are targeted at different aspects of the project: test and task.

A similar ambiguity arose concerning the run chart and the process diagram, demonstrating the ambiguous nature of SLISPs:

> The group are required to submit a run chart as part of IHI; [clinical lead] argues that there is [not] enough data to put in a run chart. [training lead] points out that it is a requirement . . . [training lead] points out that the process map shows what should happen and highlights that this doesn't happen.

From a praxiographic perspective, the PDSA and run chart are local and connected, not universal and isolated.

The ambiguities within Cohort 2's SLISP highlighted the open and contested nature of how improvement science is enacted in SLISPs. It also demonstrates how improvement science is only taken up partially in the SLISP: the run chart, as the clinical lead pointed out, did not comprise a sufficient amount of data points to demonstrate significant change. Whilst this may be accurate in a positivist sense, the training lead argued that the purpose of the run chart is for the students to become familiar with the approach, rather than actually utilising the approach itself. The training lead and the clinical lead reinforce different types of realities, but these are allowed to coexist under SLISPs. The practice of constructing a run chart, although nonsensical in a positivist sense, is acceptable as a pedagogical approach for improvement science. The PDSA unfolded a debate about 'test' and 'task'. Again, in improvement science, the PDSA is required for small tests of change; however, in the SLISP, the PDSA can be used in a broader sense to describe the stages of a task. In summary, the SLISP can be used as a way of enacting improvement science, but does not need to demonstrate improvement science as a whole approach. This demonstrates that the 'improvement' associated with the SLISP does not necessarily lead to an improvement in the workplace.

Regulating difference

In Cohort 1, the student made decisions about the SLISP, consulting with supervisory staff for guidance. In contrast, Cohort 2 were given a project by a clinical lead and then met frequently to be given more direction in the project. The enactment of improvement science in Cohort 1 was as a mindset, which came about through experience of other SLISPs. In Cohort 2, the IHI templates formed the basis of the SLISP and were adhered to. The relation between improvement science and the SLISP could be described as a partial connection (Strathern, 2005). Improvement science includes methodology, templates, and guidance to be enacted, and the SLISP includes improvement science approaches. The two approaches can be included in the other, but cannot be collapsed into a singularity. A partial connection provides an alternative to the binary of one or many, by allowing more than one and less than many.

In terms of the IHI and assessment procedures, it is inappropriate to say that we can compare like for like when it comes to improvement science projects: as has been seen by the two cases, projects can be highly diverse with a range of implications. However, we can say that these can exist together and side by side, rather than being one and the same thing. In terms of regulating difference, SLISPs are held together through narration in groups such as the IHI.

The two SLISPs demonstrate that different versions of improvement science are enacted which have implications on practice. The SLISP for Cohort 1 did not rigidly adhere to the IHI Open School practices, and aimed for longer-term change. The SLISP for Cohort 2 followed IHI procedures with the aim of implementing rapid change. In terms of ontological politics, the two SLIPs were enacting different versions of improvement science that were at odds with each other and yet coexisted in practice. The implications are that different types of learning emerged from the SLISPs that were still presented as pedagogies of improvement science. There are also implications for professional learning:

> students need to realise that professional practices are not stable, but changing, and that they need to be able to induce change in their professional work as part of their professional responsibility . . . to be able to stage and carry out processes of change, which is important, not least from the perspective of enhancing patient safety.
>
> (Dahlgren, Dahlgren and Dahlberg, 2012, p. 192)

This chapter started by exploring the enactment of SLIPs, and different practices created ambivalence of the recording of 'duration'. Despite these different enactments, the practices 'hung together' through rationalisation and translation. The choices made during the SLISP in Cohort 2 were examined as acts of ontological politics, where one reality prevailed over another through material assemblages (such as the locker and electronic equipment) and spaces (rooms and areas for group work). At first, the seemingly narrow and restrictive conditions of possibility of the SLISP through the IHI Practicum were challenged through ambiguities in the structure and elements (the PDSA cycle; a single narrative). Learning was conceptualised as distributed through space and through assemblages of objects; the students' acceptance of ambiguity and negotiating spaces created effects of learning and identity.

References

Borges, J.L. (1974). The analytical language of John Wilkins. In: R.L.C. Simms, trans., *Other Inquisitions, 1937–1952*. Austin, TX: University of Texas Press, pp. 101–105.

Dahlgren, M.A., Dahlgren, L.O. and Dahlberg, J. (2012). Learning professional practice through education. In: P. Hager, A. Lee and A. Reich, eds., *Practice, learning and change: Practice-theory perspectives on professional learning*. Dordrecht: Springer, pp. 183–197.

Fenwick, T. (2011). Reading educational reform with actor network theory: Fluid spaces, otherings, and ambivalences. *Educational Philosophy and Theory*, 43 (suppl 1), pp. 114–134.

Fenwick, T. (2014). Sociomateriality in medical practice and learning: Attuning to what matters. *Medical Education*, 48(1), pp. 44–52.

Fenwick, T. and Edwards, R. (2010). *Actor-network theory in education*. London: Routledge.

Law, J. (1994). *Organizing modernity*. Oxford: Blackwell Publishing.

Law, J. (2004). *After method: Mess in social science research*. London: Routledge.

Law, J. and Singleton, V. (2003). Allegory and its others. In: D. Nicolini, S. Gherardi and D. Yanow, eds., *Knowing in organizations: A practice-based approach*. Armonk, NY: M.E. Sharpe, pp. 225–254.

Mol, A. (2002). *The body multiple: Ontology in medical practice*. Durham: Duke University Press.

Mulcahy, D. (2014). Re-thinking teacher professional learning: More than a representational account. In: T. Fenwick and M. Nerland, eds., *Reconceptualising professional learning: Socio-material knowledges, practices and responsibilities*. Abingdon: Routledge, pp. 52–66.

Sørensen, E. (2009). *The materiality of learning: Technology and knowledge in educational practice*. Cambridge: Cambridge University Press.

Strathern, M. (2005). *Partial connections*. Walnut Creek, CA: Altamira Press.

Chapter 7

The future of ANT as methodology

In this chapter, five key points from the research are foregrounded. The points are made separately, but there is much overlap and entanglements with the other points. The key points should be considered as a way of organising and ordering the discussion by foregrounding insights that relate to the original research questions. The first key point draws out the notion of learning emerging from the potential disruption that occurs as networks collide. The second point focuses on how materials shape (or invite) practice and learning by how they are assembled and enacted. Point three highlights how the enactment of practices becomes visible through 'un-black-boxing', and how learning effects are produced through challenging singularities. Enactments of power through ontological politics are explored in the fourth point, to emphasise how learning comes about through regulating difference between different worlds of practice. Finally, the fifth point turns to the idea of human-as-assemblage, creating identities, and reconceptualising professional learning (Mitchell, 2020). These key points are then discussed in the context of COVID-19 to explore how ANT readings might create new and innovative ways of seeing how the global pandemic might be investigated.

Two anecdotes were used throughout the analysis (antimicrobial prescribing and insulin recording) and the ANT dimensions of analysis (networks, symmetry, and multiple worlds). The metaphor of networks allows the research to focus on relationality and emergence of effects rather than attributes of separate components, thereby de-centring the human to produce accounts that challenge conventional labelling, boundaries, and privileging of important actors. The notion of symmetry allows learning to be conceptualised as assemblage, turning the relationality of the network towards the spatiality of collectives of humans and non-humans. Other metaphors, such as multiple worlds, allow for alternative imaginings of learning as associations through multiple enactments (Sørensen, 2009).

Key points from the research

This research has contributed to the field in two ways: firstly, in the development of ANT as an empirical methodology, and secondly in the development of pedagogical approaches of improvement science in medical education. The methodology developed in this research demonstrates how ANT can be drawn from as a sensibility to interrupt research and to critically engage with medical education research. The research has developed the language of learning in space/time and as a relational concept, helping educators to realise that the conditions of possibility for pedagogies of improvement science can be challenged. In terms of medical and professional education, this research has contributed a detailed account of the mundane practices of SLISPs, and through description has offered critiques to the pedagogies of improvement science. Finally, this research has reconceptualised learning as networked, assembled, and contingent in different worlds of practice.

This research set out to ask: how is learning configured as students carry out the SLISPs on a hospital ward? And, how do the ANT concepts of networks, symmetry, and multiple worlds, contribute to an understanding of professional and medical education? Five key points from the research are foregrounded to address these questions. The points are made separately, but there is much overlap and entanglements with the other points. The key points should be considered as a way of organising and ordering the discussion by foregrounding insights that relate to the original research questions.

1. Conceptualising networks: learning as disruption

Through identifying and exploring actor-networks, the analysis drew attention to two things: (i) how writing about learning as a network effect rather than as an individual acquisition provides an alternative language to situate learning in space/time; and (ii) how learning can be conceptualised as an effect of the collision between new and existing networks of practice. Individualism, and the notion of the heroic individual, is prevalent in medical education (Bleakley, 2012). This has partly emerged from how doctors are expected to behave, and through discourses such as the 'character' of a 'good doctor' (Whitehead, Hodges and Austin, 2013). Calls for accountability, skills, and competence further reinforce individualism and the requirement for personal 'growth'. In this research, the idea of learning has been presented as collective and socio-material. This raises challenges to the language of learning in medical education by moving from the individual to the collective and articulating learning spatially and relationally. Learning relates to the discipline itself, and as Nespor (2014, p. 11) suggests, to the movement of the student through this discipline:

> 'Learning' (in) a discipline isn't a matter of transforming one's psychological make-up . . . Instead, 'learning' should refer to the changes in the spatial and temporal organization of the distributed actors/networks that we're always part of . . . Students enter into disciplinary practice when they begin to move along trajectories that keep them within the narrow range of space-times and distributions that constitute the discipline.

In this study, the students were considered to be part of the networks that produced learning; they were considered as being assemblages of human and non-human entities, connected to networks that valued different types of knowledge. The student could be said to be performed into being by the networks they are part of; as Latour asserts, 'entities gain their identity only through other entities' (Miettinen, 1999, p. 176). In this research, the student disciplines were medicine and pharmacy, but the notion of 'improvement' as a discipline through SLISPs was also introduced. The assemblages and distributions that characterise improvement methodologies are not the same as those that are enacted in medical and pharmaceutical practice. In addition, the clinical workplaces in which the students were leading projects are connected to well-established networks of practice that define clinical work. This suggests that the students and the networks they are connected with are coming into contact with other networks through enacting the SLISPs. The question of student learning moves from: 'what did the students learn?' and becomes: 'how do we enquire about learning from a network perspective?' In the case of this research, learning emerges from the effects that occur as the students move through networks of improvement, existing practice, and professional disciplines. In addition to networks, an emphasis on symmetry, through assemblages of human and non-human actants and the relations between actants, provides another metaphor to describe learning as socio-material. The concept of learning as assemblage incorporates the social (e.g. negotiations around meaning and knowledge within groups) and the material (spaces, objects, etc.). In this version, learning is relational, with the focus on:

> associations, or connections, or relations through which matter and meaning, object and subject, co-emerge . . . learning achieves its form as a consequence of the relations in which it is located and enacted.
>
> (Mulcahy, 2014, p. 56)

The antibiotic story network and the sticker network presented ways of articulating learning as an effect produced beyond the individual and enmeshed in workplace practice. Another contribution of the network metaphor is that of stability, movement and strength: in classic-ANT, networks become stable when the performances that support them are repeated, and the forces that make connections are strengthened. Networks then become mobilised and form connections with other networks. An important consideration is that continuous work is required for this stability; networks can become destabilised or disrupted by performing practices from other networks, or through resistances or reform. All these considerations are relevant to improvement science and how this has become enacted in SLISPs.

The network metaphor allows for SLISPs to be reconceptualised, moving from a benevolent 'improvement' in patient care, towards a potentially disruptive intervention to everyday practice. This study has demonstrated that it is a fine balance between improving practices and disrupting work. However, if no improvements are made there is a risk that practices may lead to harm, such as inaccurate prescribing of antibiotics leading to kidney infection, or inaccurate prescribing of insulin leading to hypoglycaemia. To make a meaningful improvement the new practice needs to take hold, to build connections, and to be performed repeatedly, aligning, and ordering materials to support this new practice. If this is not achieved, the improvement will not take root and the network will disintegrate. However, the value for the students is in the formation and breakage of connections, as the learning has the potential for disruption: it might not make for consistency, but the students are able to attune to what matters for them and their SLISP (Fenwick, 2014b) and to understand the complexities for implementing change. Allen (2013) demonstrated through research into the implementation of Integrated Care Pathways (ICP) that innovations and improvements can be disruptive to practices, creating new problems. For example, in Cohort 2 the sticker added more boxes for information relating to insulin. Even though there was staff support and evidence to support collecting additional information, this required a change in practice that was potentially disruptive.

For Cohort 1 improvement science was regarded as a 'mindset' with a weak connection to the IHI Practicum templates. The implication for Cohort 1 was that connections and associations had been made in practice over time and that new networks had formed, with the IHI network retreating and new 'improvement' networks stabilising or mutating (Fenwick and Edwards, 2010). The new connections for Cohort 1 suggest learning emerged as effects from the changed configuration and organisation of the new networks. For Cohort 2, learning effects were distributed in the configuration of SLISP practices, for example, in the fishbone diagram. SLISPs provide a way of mobilising improvement science methodologies, alongside promoting the student as a leader and change agent (Paterson et al., 2011). This has implications for the role of the professional. Improvement science, as a healthcare improvement innovation, is enacted by internal and external networks. This research does not claim to act as an evaluation for either SLISPs or improvement science (for an evaluation of improvement science in nurse education, see Armstrong, Lauder and Shepherd, 2015), but provides an interruption to the assumptions and deletions that have already begun in relation to improvement science. This research argues that instead of establishing a 'common language' it is more useful to explore how improvement science is enacted in practice.

At the start of this study, it was recognised that SLISPs offer students a new way of learning that is situated in workplace practice. Current approaches to learning in healthcare (and many other areas) are focused on individual acquisition, for example measuring competencies, attributes, skills, and attitude. A different approach to learning is required that can accommodate changing values in the NHS in the move towards interdisciplinarity and teamwork (Bleakley, 2014), which brings different networks into contact, creating new networks and disrupting existing ones. ANT offers an alternative language for educators by describing learning as situated, distributed and enmeshed.

2. Materials inviting practice

The focus of this section is the notion of objects 'inviting' practice. The choice of language draws from discussions on how an ANT sensibility influences terms and descriptions. For example, Abrahamsson et al. (2015) present the terms 'affording, responding, caring and tinkering' to replace more commonly used terms such as 'causing' and 'acting'. Fenwick (Fenwick, 2014b) suggests the use of the terms 'attending, attuning, noticing, tinkering and interrupting' specifically in relation to medical education. In this section, the term 'inviting' in relation to practice is included to encompass Latour's ideas of technical mediation (Latour, 1999) and Fenwick and Edwards' (2010) descriptions of the socio-material in education. There are examples in the literature of how materials invite or shape practice. Latour, writing as Johnson (Johnson, 1988), describes how the door-closer 'programs' the human as they take passage through the door: the human is 'coded' to walk at a certain pace, to avoid either having to squeeze through a narrow space if they approach the door too soon, or having the door shut in their face to give them a bloody nose. This is an example of how materials influence behaviour, and describes the move away from the idea of human agency which is prevalent in the social sciences. Latour (1999) describes relations in human and non-human collectives as shaping reality: objects and humans do not exist separately, but collectively and relation to one another. As has been demonstrated in this research, detailed descriptions of everyday practice are therefore necessary to attune to these relations and practices. Because of this, some authors argue that ANT accounts can be mundane and irrelevant (Collins and Yearly, 1992). However, in the hospital, the students were required to negotiate corridors, stairs, the buzzer system, the bleep system, the locker room, and clinical spaces; although time-consuming, these practices formed how the SLISPs were carried out and highlighted the importance of recording detail. In Cohort 1, locating paperwork on the wards, negotiating the space of the wards, and the manipulation of materials, were time-consuming and seemingly repetitive practices that might not have appeared significant in the practices of the SLISP. However, the performance of the student collecting information brought attention to how material assemblages came together and created effects (Fenwick and Edwards, 2010).

The physical shapes of actants invited or excluded practice, for example, trolleys for transporting multiple ring binders contrasted with cumbersome double clipboards that resisted being stacked and transported en masse. The materialities of each ward were unique and contingent, and could not have been replicated in a classroom or simulation. Although medical and pharmacy students are taught about dexterity relating to the clinical and medical aspects of their roles (Bleakley, Bligh and Browne, 2011), it is difficult to justify teaching how to juggle paperwork, pens, stationary, and so on, despite this being a crucial part of the job. The students became familiar with materiality by being present on the wards during, for example, ward rounds, but the SLISPs enabled students to physically work with paperwork and to form connections with patient information.

Material properties, such as colour, were powerful actants on the ward. For example, the red bar across the gentamycin chart allowed it to stand out against the prescription chart and makes it less likely to misplace; the pink colour of forms relating to insulin use was copied for the sticker, to associate it with insulin prescribing procedures. In the example of the insulin sticker, forces, and effects became evident through its enactment in the SLISP. The co-emergence of matter and meaning (Mulcahy, 2014), through the increased power that the sticker was collecting through various enactments, was evident in the increased presence of the sticker on forms in the wards. The secret drawer demonstrated how the assemblage of entities influenced the SLISP and the performance of the sticker in relation to the 'improvement'. In another example, the locker presented how assemblages of human and non-human entities come together to shape practice. The online practices in Cohort 2 was another example of how the SLISP was driven through material configurations that subscribed to electronic media. An early commitment to electronic templates created greater forces through online forums and closed media sharing repositories. The location and use of the locker, the distribution of materials across floors and the distribution of the students, commuting via trains and buses, all contributed to how the SLISP was enacted.

In both SLISPs, spaces were occupied for practices they were not explicitly invited to undertake or spaces designated for specific activities were not conducive to those practices. For Cohort 2, the locker room performed many spaces, including the project work, meetings/handovers, and storage both inside and outside the actual locker. There was one small bench in the locker room, but no other furniture, so when the students used the space for sticking on stickers other objects were used as furniture: an umbrella, an iPad, a lap, the floor. Although teaching rooms were designed for the purpose of student working, there were booking systems that sometimes prevented these from being enacted as learning spaces for the SLISP. The access (buzzer) system for the pharmacy offices prevented use as a learning or meeting place. The buzzer system was identified in ANT terms as an Obligatory Passage Point (OPP) in the analysis. Identifying OPPs are useful for understanding where the bottle-necks occur in practices, and what can slow practices down.

These examples highlight how materials can drive and shape practice, and how SLISPs need to be attuned to the socio-material practices of workplace learning. Attuning to these invitations helps the researcher to notice how learning emerges from assembling and ordering both human and non-human entities, and how this results in patterns of practice that are not purely consciously controlled by humans. This addresses some of the critiques of ANT and highlights how ANT differs from other socio-material approaches such as complexity theory and CHAT.

3. Invisible, black-boxed practices

There are a number of ways in which practices might become invisible that relate to the three ANT dimensions foregrounded in this analysis. First, the notion of networks and focus on relations between actors might foreground more powerful actors and bracket others: this highlights the importance of analysing networks by recognising less prominent actants, and to focus instead on effects and relations. Inscription devices, systems that translate knowledge from one form to another, can also be identified within networks to identify minute points of translation that might otherwise be hidden (Latour and Woolgar, 2013). Second, the work involved in sustaining mundane practices sometimes leads to practices being taken for granted or black-boxed: a symmetrical approach provides a way of attending to the everyday detail and making processes visible again. Thirdly, conceptualising the multiple from a singularity also opens out the complexity of practice. This can be achieved by seeing 'matters of fact' as 'matters of concern' (Latour, 2005). Praxiography (Mol, 2002) is an empirical approach to holding open controversies and conceptualising multiple worlds. From Mol (2002), Law's descriptions of regulating difference provide examples of how different worlds can exist together, or how one world can dominate through ontological politics (Law, 2004b).

Throughout the research there were examples of how practices were taken for granted or 'black-boxed'. The SLISPs provided a way of prising open the black boxes, by approaching the familiar as strange; for example, the pharmacy students from Cohort 2 voiced their surprise when encountering practices on the ward, and the tour of the surgical 'floor' re-presented the separate surgical wards. In the example of the sticker, the configuration of the pharmacy offices and materiality of the buzzer system to gain entry, all conspired to influence the way in which the SLISP was carried out. However, in everyday practice, the bleep and buzzer systems may not be considered important, as these have been mastered by experienced staff. These practices become deleted, much like the magic trick of sawing the woman in two (Chapter 5): the woman in the box hides her contortions, creating the illusion that the saw is going through the middle of her body. The deletions that make magic tricks possible, that is, assumptions of what is capable of acting (in the case of humanism and socio-cultural approaches, humans are the only agents) enable practices to become invisible and deleted. There are other ways in which some things become invisible: attending to what is considered important and made present, results in absences. And, as Latour (1999) noted, by ascribing purposeful action and intention to humans, the contribution of objects in processes can go unnoticed. Criticisms aimed at early-ANT conceptualisations of networks were that they foregrounded the most powerful actors (Fenwick and Edwards, 2010; McLean and Hassard, 2004), and overlooked others. This illustrates how networks can also make some practices invisible because of a priori assumptions about what is important. This is particularly significant when researching workplace and professional education, where everyday detail contributes to practice and learning in myriad different ways. The implications of error in clinical working are considerable. The example of the sticky strip on the gentamycin form is an illustration of this: stationery might not be considered important compared to medicines, but when a gentamycin form is lost, the patient is a risk of receiving a harmful double dose, leading to kidney infection. Similarly, the lack of information relating to insulin prescribing on the medical reconciliation form might lead to hypoglycaemia.

The process of bracketing practices through inscription devices is explored by Latour and Woolgar (2013). These devices are configurations of materials that transform material into text, such as a blood test to prescribe the correct dose of gentamycin. These systems delete practices until all that is left is the result or process which defines the limits of practice. In Latour and Woolgar's (2013) exploration, the focus is the construction of scientific papers through laboratory practices, but there are analogies to working practices on the hospital ward. Latour's (2005) notion of 'matters of fact and matters of concern' refer to a premature unification of things that are closed down into a singularity. Improvement science might be an example of this, where the complexities, disputes, and controversies are either glossed over or bracketed. 'Matters of concern' come about when complexity is allowed to open out. In this research, the buzzer system has been collapsed into a singularity of practice, but the observations allowed the assemblage of associated practices such as waiting, the door, the clinical lead, to be explored in detail. The challenge with this approach is knowing when to stop: Latour (2005) describes this using Zeno's paradoxes, where the continual process of unfolding slows everything down to an absurd rate.

It is commonplace and necessary to delete the work and effort that goes into practices as a way of ordering work and producing procedures and protocols. However, SLISPs enable other things to become present and absent, to question the limits of possibility. For example, the buzzer system for the pharmacy offices was not included in the induction presentation for Cohort 2, neither was the process of making the stickers or booking teaching rooms. However, these were the working practices that shaped Cohort 2's SLISP. The implications of this are that much of the work of the SLISP becomes invisible when the IHI Practicum report is produced, even though this deleted work may be of value to future projects. Instead, the templates (PDSA forms, run charts, and so on) act as the mouthpiece for SLISP activity. The enactment of improvement science as a healthcare innovation can be understood differently with an ANT lens. This research has articulated a way in which hidden work can be made visible. The example of duration in Cohort 1 focuses on multiplicity and multiple ontologies (Mol, 2002), drawing out the different ways in which multiple worlds can be conceptualised as either layered, drawn together, converted, rationalised, or dominant. Law's (2004b) interpretation of 'regulating difference', following Mol's (2002) praxiography, demonstrates how the different recordings of duration were held together in practice through translations, where information is converted for different practices, and how the supervisor meeting rationalised duration, explaining away difference through dialogue.

In this study, improvement science could be considered as an example of an intervention that has been packaged and transported as an immutable mobile to different settings, with an expectation of consistent results. Immutable mobiles can be defined as stable actants which hold their shape of relations so that they can be transported without changing. However, as has been demonstrated in the literature around the WHO surgical safety checklist, mobilisation brings with it translation, which is ultimately treason and betrayal (Law, 2006). In other words, if an entity is expected to perform in exactly the same way in a different context, then this can lead to unexpected effects as new associations reconstruct the entity in a different way. Studies on new innovations that are packaged and measured as a consistent 'thing' are therefore problematic, as the 'thing' shifts and mutates according to the networks it becomes associated with. This study confronts the shifting, mutating mass as a dynamic process of relations, associations, and connections that can be noticed when attuning to workplace practices – not just through the behaviour and actions of humans, but in the chains of translations in heterogeneous assemblages of human and non-human entities. There is a risk that approaches such as improvement science become automatised uncritically (Law, 2004b), leading to the assumption that it will have the same effects in different circumstances. This research has presented improvement science as a way of un-black-boxing activities and processes to explore invisible practices that might otherwise be overlooked.

4. Ontological politics of learning: regulating difference

The previous points begin to explore issues of power through the lens of ANT. As Fenwick and Nimmo (2015, p. 78) point out:

> sociomaterial perspectives offer important approaches for understanding the power relations and politics that constitute learning. Their analytical tools can interrupt and trace the ways powerful webs become assembled as knowledge, but also point to affirmative ways to interne in, disturb or amplify these.

The concept of powerful discourses, particularly those of selling and resistance, has also been explored in this study. However, it has been argued that hegemonic discourses are derived from human-centred traditions and, as such, focus on the social more than the material (Fenwick, Edwards and Sawchuk, 2011). In this research, the discourses of selling and resistance were identified as network effects (sometimes resistance, sometimes alliance). This is an important consideration as there is a risk that discourses are privileged above other, more material effects, such as the configuration of paperwork and stationery.

The concept of multiple worlds enabled several issues to be drawn out in relation to learning. First, ambivalence and difference were pursued in the data: ANT looks down into the data, into the baroque curlicues of the detail of practice, finding openings through ambiguity (Law, 2004a). Second, the idea of multiplicity is presented: not of multiple perspectives, views, and subjectivities of the same 'object', and not of fracturing a singular object into multiple pieces, but something in-between: more than one and less than many (Law, 2004b). With the example of duration, the seemingly singular recording unfolds into multiple practices of medicinal prescribing, monitoring, and administering; but rather than fracturing 'duration', the practices function together. This brings a third notion of multiple worlds: the practices of duration exist in different worlds, which function side by side. These worlds are performed into being and shaped by practice. Fourth, where worlds exist side by side, some might become dominant and others are lashed together through rationalisation or narrative. These 'regulating differences' are acts of ontological politics (Mol, 1998), the decisions that are made to shape a world, coming from priorities, authority, and professional judgement. In healthcare, the idea of a 'common language' is a way of rationalising difference in an attempt to smooth out inconsistencies and to produce an unchangeable entity that can be transported without change: in ANT terms, an immutable mobile.

The distribution of power and authority was explored through the recording of 'duration'. The tensions and strain (Fenwick and Edwards, 2010) that were created through ambiguous recordings of duration signposted to different worlds of practice. The record for 'duration' became a multiplicity with relations in multiple worlds. The enactments of practices around duration connected to different worlds for different roles: the nurse is connected to the administration of medication and the medication trolley; the junior doctor relates practice to medical training, protocols, decisions made by the registrar, patient test readings and so on. For Cohort 1, duration became a balance between clinical judgement and protocol, resulting in ambiguity in the records. Authority and power arose in the negotiations that took place in recording duration, as practices highlighted minute translations which deviated from protocol with the purpose of exercising clinical judgement. The duration example draws from Mol's (2002) multiple worlds to demonstrate how practices and roles enact duration from the same prescription form. The power of the prevalent world can supress other versions and set the conditions of possibility. Star (1990) quotes Everett Hughes' 'it might have been otherwise' to describe how some versions are supressed through history and how some prevail, such as the red colour of a traffic light signalling 'stop'; the red colour was a choice, not an innate symbolism of the colour red to prompt stopping. In a similar way, insulin recording forms for Cohort 2 were associated with the colour pink.

The current version, the 'way we do things', might not be the only way; existing practices might 'improve' with the introduction of a SLISP, but the change
itself is disruptive. Improvement science methodology addresses this through
'balancing measures' to anticipate 'unintended consequences' but this could be
construed as an oversimplification of complex social practices.

The anecdote of Cohort 2's project, through the IHI Practicum, enacts
improvement science as rapid change; however, Cohort 1's SLISP demonstrates
how improvement science is employed to implement change over a longer
period of time. In terms of 'what is at stake' with these two versions, rapid
change might sacrifice detail, and longer change might sacrifice responsive-
ness and timeliness. It is beyond the scope of this study to argue in favour
of either version, as might be the case in an evaluation. Rather, this study
highlights the ontological politics that take place in the enactment of improvement science and what the implications of this are on learning. In the case of
Cohort 2, learning emerges through practices of the IHI Practicum and the
electronic format of the SLISP report; different worlds may have been created
through manual approaches that may have produced different learning effects.
For Cohort 1, learning was enmeshed in the practices of antibiotic prescribing,
with improvement science as a mindset being introduced to these practices.
Again, different worlds may have been created through a more rigid application
of IHI templates: a 'network of prescription' rather than a 'network of negotiation' (Fenwick and Edwards, 2010) with different learning emerging as a result.

5. Assembling realities

During the fieldwork and analysis, the concept of professionalism and membership emerged in the assemblages of materials that signified a nurse, doctor,
patient, and so on. For example, the uniforms, lanyards, and comportment of
bodies identified the ambulating blue-clothed body as 'nurse', while the prone
body in a bed with plastic tubes and IV stands as 'patient'. Throughout the
fieldwork and analysis, the patient became recognised as a manifest absence
(Law, 2004b). The embodied patient may have been absent, but the patients
themselves were present in other ways: distributed through paperwork, in different parts of the ward. Mol (2002) describes the 'fleshiness' of the patient
body, its different 'layers' and that a body may be multiple without being plural.
Star (1990) has also highlighted the notion of multiple membership, and how
a self can be distributed through different networks. The antibiotic story of the
patient was connected in different places to different networks. The work of
the SLISP was to make new connections and associations, but in doing so, the
information went through points of translation. This process highlighted the
contingent nature of information, for example, recording patient notes (Berg
and Goorman, 1999), and how new networks began to form alongside existing
practices. The meaning of the antibiotic story was a new reality, a new set of
associations and assemblages, rather than a representation of the patient. The

antibiotic story crafted the patient and performed their reality into being. In Cohort 1, the antibiotic story was about associating and connecting in new ways, resulting in learning effects. The network metaphor worked well in conceptualising the SLISP as a new network, and how overlapping connections sought to disrupt and rupture (Fenwick and Edwards, 2010) existing practices to introduce the 'improvement'. From the anecdotes in this study and other ethnographies, there is an argument against the potential amorality perceived in de-centring the human (Pels, 1996). In this study, the human is present in ANT accounts, but in a range of manifestations that challenge embodiment as a singularity and present the patient as dispersed.

Other assemblages were explored in the research, relating to the different professions of hospital staff. It became clear that the differences between roles were more complex than simply the allocation of practices. Staff rotation (junior doctors), shift working, being located in one ward (nurses, doctors) at a time or several at the same time (pharmacists) created effects on practices and spaces. The SLISP introduced a new set of practices to the students which cut across some of the boundaries created by roles. There was an emphasis, from the student supervisors, on interdisciplinary working. This was aimed towards clinical teams and professional learning, and in Cohort 2, the interdisciplinary aspect extended to the students themselves. The implications of interdisciplinary working are that there are networks colliding and destabilising to accommodate different ways of working. An observation from the study is the way that a single object (such as a clipboard or the prescription chart) can signpost different worlds of practice. The handling of materials signposted to diverse practices: the student was recording information for the purposes of improvement, whereas the nurse was checking information to treat a patient. The prescription chart was an interesting example of how objects connected with practice. In my study, nurses referred to the prescription chart as a 'Kardex' or 'X-PAR'. These descriptions explicitly include the administration role (X-PAR stands for X-Health board; Prescription and Administration Record). Pharmacists use the term 'prescription chart', a term which black-boxes administration and recording. The medical students usually referred to the X-PAR, but sometimes used the other terms. In the example of recording 'duration', the different practices of prescribing, administering, and reviewing duration were all under the same label. The significance of this is how practices perform a label into being; repeated performance strengthens the identity of that practice. In different disciplines, the same referent performs differently. The SLISP became a way of performing improvement science; the twin purposes of 'students as change agents' and rapid improvement are strongly connected in a network of practices that includes the IHI Practicum and the endorsement of senior clinical staff. However, it is likely that there is much diversity under this banner that will be unrecognised from the deletion of practices to reduce activities to a SLISP.

The interdisciplinary aspect of the SLISPs was emphasised and encouraged, particularly in Cohort 2. There is a shift towards interdisciplinary practices in healthcare (Ahn et al., 2015; Bleakley, Bligh and Browne, 2011) that has implications for working practices. This study has highlighted how networks are formed through practices of different disciplines, and also the potential disruption change can have in destabilising these networks. Repeated enactments cause practices to be deleted, shaping the world of the discipline through ontological politics. The difference between worlds can mean that some ideas are alien or even absurd: the way that the clinical space of the surgical floor is conceptualised challenges the confines of the ward; working patterns create different practices such as the 'secret drawer'; recording duration produces ambiguities that have different implications in different practices. The SLISP, as a new network forming, illuminates some of these absurdities and presses for change and 'improvement'; counter-forces preserve practices with the logic of the discipline. The implications are that 'improvement' is not a consistent change that will have the same effects on different networks of practice, but will be enacted differently in different worlds. For the students, working towards inter-disciplinarity creates destabilising effects but can challenge the conditions of possibility in working practices. An effect of these intersecting worlds is that learning is reconceptualised as collective, situated, and contingent in practice.

Educational implications

Traditionally, learning is measured as an individual attribute that has accumulated because of increased knowledge. This study moves away from such assumptions, to conceptualise learning and knowledge as effects in space/time (Nespor, 2014) and as dispersed (Mol, 2002; Sørensen, 2009). Rather than saying: 'this is what the students learned whilst doing the SLISPs', we could say that they have become part of new networks, performed connections and relations to networks, become part of an assemblage of human and non-human actants that enact improvement science, and have become attuned to the different worlds that hang together under the banner of patient care. Therefore, learning, as an effect of the SLISP network, is manifest in the repeated negotiations of clinical space, the reconceptualisation of spaces and the acceptance of different worlds that hang together to create reality: practice precedes reality, and the enactment of improvement science has created multiple realities. The question changes from: how effective is improvement science or SLISPs in terms of student learning? to: what reality has gained more ground and what political decisions got us there? The focus of this research was on professional learning. Interdisciplinary-working, team-working, and co-production are all considerations of professional learning, and these aspects have been investigated as part of socio-material practices in medical education (Bleakley, Bligh and Browne, 2011; McMurtry, Rohse and Kilgour, 2016) and other areas of professional education (Fenwick and Nerland, 2014). The implications of this research are to further press for socio-material conceptualisations of professional learning, with the purpose of gaining a different understanding of how practices in the workplace are enacted and how learning is situated and contingent rather than individual and psychologised.

The implications were that learning was conceptualised through connections, rather than a linear progression from what is unknown to known, culminating in accumulated learning. The connections themselves were enacted through practices whilst carrying out the SLISP. In this study, symmetry provided a way of observing practice as relational. Treating human and non-human elements of the network equally can lead to noticing details of practice, significant to learning, which might otherwise be overlooked. In the case of this study, symmetry allowed for noticing how materials such as ring binders and clipboards invited or excluded practice, shaping the activities for the student carrying out the SLISP. Learning is conceptualised as situated and dispersed through heterogenous assemblages of human and non-human entities such as the gentamycin form, ring binders, paperwork, and clinical spaces. Finally, instead of collapsing improvement science into a 'common language', multiple worlds allowed for different enactments of improvement science to co-exist, to challenge the conditions of possibility. In the analytic example, the recording of duration was identified as an ambiguity that pointed to diverse practices on the ward that 'hung together' (Mol, 2002) around the same document (the prescription chart). For Cohort 1, learning was contingent in the meanings suspended between worlds, rather than in the reconciliation of diverse practices into a singularity.

ANT and COVID-19

The 'network' in ANT is more about how people and things come together and form connections so that actions can take place. It is about including the non-human in our systems, and recognising the role these objects play, which may be different in different networks. We can see the new networks that are arising through social distancing, where the connections with travel and transport are declining and becoming weaker. At the time of writing, public transport and car travel have been greatly reduced in the UK. Where vehicles were once prominent actants, the roads and rails that carried them and the fuel that sustained them, now belong in different networks to our working ones.

The notion of symmetry can also help us to trace the global pandemic as the virus was carried, not just by people, but by animals, planes, trains and public spaces. Without transport, the virus would not have spread so quickly around the world. And after the detection of the virus, we witnessed different countries taking different measures with Personal Protective Equipment (PPE) and testing regimes. Drawing from ANT, we could comment on how PPE provided a barrier for the virus, but how the virus could thwart our efforts if not enough protection was provided, or changed frequently enough. The material aspects of COVID-19 were very keenly felt in severe cases, through intubation and the aggressive use of ventilators to sustain life. With regards the key point of 'materials inviting practice', we can start to appreciate the agency of materials, and the diasporic nature of the human condition. We become vectors, sometimes asymptomatic as the virus invisibly travels within us.

Invisible, black-boxed practices become exposed in the changes that have come about with COVID-19. Matters that were settled have now become matters of concern. The emphasis on testing in some countries has proved to be an important measure for stopping the spread of the virus. However, in countries (like the UK) where widespread testing has not been implemented as thoroughly, the human population remain 'matters of concern', particularly humans (staff and patients) within the health service, who may or may not be carrying and transmitting the virus. The uncertainty and invisibility lead to further spreading, and it is evident this is a black-box that needs to be unpacked.

The idea of multiple worlds brings the alternative performances of COVID-19 to light. Rather than different perspectives, we have experienced how different enactments have created realities for COVID-19. Through powerful discourses, the media and politics present the virus as something to be contained or contracted. The latter discourse, introduced to the UK as 'herd immunity' suggested the majority of the population would be exposed to the virus to enable a critical mass of people to develop immunity. However, what countries around the world learned, was that it was not so much the effect of the virus (most only develop mild symptoms and it was considered by some to be just a bad case of flu), but the volume of cases presented in a short space of time and their subsequent need for treatment. The fight against coronavirus became logistical and situated in healthcare capacity. The idea of 'herd immunity' became a collateral reality (Law, 2009), no longer a viable option due to the number of deaths and requirement for mass treatment. A consensus of sorts was reached by regulating difference between these conflicting worlds of truth and by presenting an overarching narrative that was about how society copes with exponentially increasing numbers of casualties, rather than arguing about the severity of the illness in comparison with other illnesses.

The assembled realities of COVID-19 became evident in new configurations of medical practice, one dominated by the ominous coverings of dehumanising PPE; plastic facemasks, blue gloves, gowns, and aprons. Ventilators, like PPE – in short supply, became an OPP between life and death. Social distancing created new configurations of gatherings, modelled on TV with presenters sitting two metres apart, in supermarkets with huge spaced-out queues and milling customers who focused on the task in hand rather than browsing and procrastinating. Online platforms such as Zoom, Google meet, Skype, and streaming video from house to house became a mainstay for isolating individuals and households. Although the technology has been available for many years, it is now a powerful actor in the quest for social bonding and belonging, in a time when touching is now taboo.

ANT as methodology

This research has brought to light the physicality of enacting SLISPs, through manipulating forms and stationery; electronic hardware and software; negotiating corridors, stairs, and doors; and taken-for-granted procedures such as the buzzer system. It has shown how the learning effects of the SLISPs bring new aspects to the professional role of the students, such as interrupting, disrupting, and challenging existing practices as part of clinical work. This raises the question of what is at stake as students take on the role of improver and leader as well as clinician: the professional role might be viewed as more interdisciplinary, and what might be at stake is specialism and expertise. More broadly, this research explored how innovation and change can be introduced to existing practices and the effects these have, particularly the learning effects. The network metaphor is helpful in conceptualising the strength of existing networks to sustain everyday practice, and how resistances to change can make it difficult to implement improvements. Multiple worlds highlighted how multiple practices exist alongside each other but might not be commensurate with each other. In this scenario, as demonstrated through the recording of 'duration', 'improvement' may be greater in some areas than others. Indeed, this is what Allen (2013) found when investigating ICP; the codified format suited some practitioners, but the nuances and variation in other practices were not easily integrated into the new way of recording.

This research was considered to be a timely interruption to the improvement science literature. Other innovations might also benefit from the form of detailed analysis ANT has to offer. For example, the World Health Organisation (WHO) Surgical Safety Checklist (SSC) was introduced as a healthcare improvement in 2008. The research conducted on the SSC has been largely quantitative which has led to the proliferation of replication studies, producing varying results. A study of the SSC literature concluded that, rather than knowledge becoming mobilised to inform policy decisions, the evidence has come to a standstill (Mitchell et al., 2017). An open letter to The BMJ conveyed the strength of feeling in the medical community about the need to draw from more qualitative studies in order to make meaningful decisions (Greenhalgh et al., 2016). In this case, ANT could provide a robust and complementary research methodology. In evidence-based healthcare interventions (such as the surgical safety checklist and improvement science), there is sometimes a tendency to homogenise the intervention to allow for evaluation and measurement. However, this research argues that matter and meaning emerge as a result of different associations in different worlds, and that these should be more closely scrutinised alongside evaluation. In addition, as healthcare moves towards interdisciplinary-working and team-working, individualised learning approaches relating to competencies, skills, and attributes need to be superseded by more collective, socio-material readings of learning. ANT also provides a way of challenging categories and boundaries by identifying assemblages that are associated through practices.

Living through the coronavirus pandemic of 2020 gives the opportunity for many lessons to be learned. It is likely the outbreak will change global societies, as economic disaster lies in its wake. At present, we are still living through the phenomenon, and wait to see if social distancing will be enough to reduce cases and stave off the virus, or of secondary peaks occur once society goes back to living the way it did before the outbreak. There is the possibility of lockdown for weeks, if not months to come, and some speculate we will never be the same again. If ever there was a need for ANT, it is now. It has become more important than ever to notice and attend to the new configurations of being, and to trace the learning that arises from these massive changes.

ANT and medical education

There has been a growing interest in socio-materiality in researching medical education (Fenwick and Nimmo, 2015; McMurtry, Rohse and Kilgour, 2016). This research has led to a more detailed knowledge of improvement science practices in situ; medical educators are better informed of practices undertaken by students during SLISPs. Pedagogies of improvement science include class-room lectures, eLearning (through the IHI Open School Practicum), super-vision guidance, and workplace learning. This research has described how these assemble and the importance of situated learning in the workplace. The research also addresses the appropriateness of different pedagogical approaches and the implications of these. There is a degree of incommensurability and disruption which contributes to the learning process. Different meanings reside in different worlds, and this is difficult to measure or articulate. Improvement science becomes a synecdoche (where a part represents the whole) of the SLISP, with one part describing the whole process and deleting other parts. Along with multiple worlds is the acceptance that entities exist only alongside other entities, so improvement science becomes associated with different entities in different worlds. This challenges the idea of a 'common language' as terms take on different meanings in different worlds.

The pedagogical approach for learning improvement science was to create student-led projects in workplace settings to allow students to work unsupervised and to make decisions relating to the improvement. What the research has demonstrated in relation to this, is that the workplace setting is crucial in order to appreciate networks of existing practices; although simulation is becoming a popular pedagogic approach in medical education and pharmacy (Bleakley, 2014; Buchan et al., 2014), improvement is an area where workplace practice is beneficial. However, as the analysis suggests, improvement requires an engagement with, and a disruption to, existing networks of practice. The students undertook eLearning modules through the IHI Practicum prior to starting their projects, and Cohort 2 received some classroom-based instruction and guidance before entering the wards and on their first visit. These activities created the effects of power as students came onto the wards to collect information and canvass staff about their improvement projects. As the SLISPs were enacted, connections and associations formed a network which interacted with existing networks of practice on the wards.

Interdisciplinary working is becoming more widely promoted in the NHS as a way of working (Bleakley, 2012, 2014; Falk, Hopwood and Dahlgren, 2017; Fenwick, 2014a; McMurtry, Rohse and Kilgour, 2016). It has been argued that the learning that accompanies these ways of working needs to be consistent with shared working procedures rather than individualised competencies and skills (Bleakley, 2014). It is challenging to move away from individual attributes in the context of exams and personal achievements; the language of learning is also embroiled in individualism, with terms such as 'skills' still prevalent in the current improvement science literature (Gabbay et al., 2014; Lucas and Nacer, 2015). The social perspective, as introduced by Mulcahy's (2014) three tales of learning, introduces an alternative to cognitive, psychologised approaches to learning by discussing learning as part of a collective and situated in practice. The socio-material perspective extends this to include assemblages of humans and non-humans that form relations and practices, with learning as an effect emerging from these interactions. In this research, learning has been described from the network metaphor as an effect of connections, and from the symmetry perspective as the ordering and assembling of human and non-human entities. Learning is also described as contingent meanings in multiple worlds that co-exist in practices. De-centring the human allows for descriptions of learning in the workplace that bypass the predilection for exploring motivations and intention, social structures, and human agency. In terms of professional learning, this research has connected practice and learning and moved away from conceptualising learning as cognitive and acquisitional. This expands the lexicon for learning, and allows for social and material imaginings of workplace learning.

Conclusion

This study investigated learning as socio-material, drawing from ANT to conceptualise learning as a network effect. The pedagogies of improvement science took the student away from the classroom and individual examinations, and into the world of live practice, interdisciplinary work, teamwork, and all the complexity that goes with this. Interconnections and associations were described through observing practice and then 'following the actor' as an entry point to the data. The three ANT concepts contribute to medical education in the following ways: first, networks can help educators conceptualise learning as dynamic, contingent, and complex; pedagogies of improvement science can be adapted to help students appreciate the mess without attempting to capture the whole. Second, symmetry can help students and educators to see what would otherwise be overlooked: by challenging the assumption that humans are the sole source of agency, the human is decentred and more relational conceptualisations can be accessed. Finally, accepting the existence of multiple worlds that co-exist without pulling everything, including improvement science, into a singularity, can help educators to appreciate multiplicities without having to reduce them. As well as providing insights for improvement science practices in the NHS, this research challenges the conditions of possibility for how innovations are enacted in the workplace, and how changes to society and medicine, such as the COVID-19 outbreak, create new worlds.

References

Abrahamsson, S., Bertoni, F., Mol, A. and Martín, R.I. (2015). Living with omega-3: New materialism and enduring concerns. *Environment and Planning D: Society and Space*, 33(1), pp. 4–19.

Ahn, S., Rimpiläinen, S., Theodorsson, A., Fenwick, T. and Dahlgren, M.A. (2015). Learning in technology-enhanced medical simulation: Locations and knowings. *Professions and Professionalism*, 5(3).

Allen, D. (2013). Understanding context for quality improvement: Artefacts, affordances and socio-material infrastructure. *Health*, 17(5), pp. 460–477.

Armstrong, L., Lauder, W. and Shepherd, A. (2015). An evaluation of methods used to teach quality improvement to undergraduate healthcare students to inform curriculum development within preregistration nurse education: A protocol for systematic review and narrative synthesis. *Systematic Reviews*, 4(1), pp. 8.

Berg, M. and Goorman, E. (1999). The contextual nature of medical information. *International Journal of Medical Informatics*, 56(1), pp. 51–60.

Bleakley, A. (2012). The proof is in the pudding: Putting actor-network-theory to work in medical education. *Medical Teacher*, 34(6), pp. 462–467.

Bleakley, A. (2014). *Patient-centred medicine in transition: The heart of the matter*. Vol. 3. Heidelberg: Springer Science & Business Media.

Bleakley, A., Bligh, J. and Browne, J. (2011). *Medical education for the future: Identity, power and location*. Heidelberg: Springer Science & Business Media.

Buchan, S., Regan, K., Filion-Murphy, C., Little, K., Strath, A., Rowe, I. and Vosper, H. (2014). Students as partners in a quality improvement approach to learning enhancement: A case study from a pharmacy undergraduate course. *Communicare*, 1(1).

Collins, H. and Yearly, S. (1992). Epistemological chicken. In: A. Pickering, ed., *Science as practice and culture*. Chicago, IL: The University of Chicago Press, pp. 301–326.

Falk, A.L., Hopwood, N. and Dahlgren, M.A. (2017). Unfolding practices: A sociomaterial View of interprofessional collaboration in health care. *Professions and Professionalism*, 7(2).

Fenwick, T. (2014a). Knowledge circulations in inter-para/professional practice: A sociomaterial enquiry. *Journal of Vocational Education & Training*, 66(3), pp. 264–280.

Fenwick, T. (2014b). Sociomateriality in medical practice and learning: Attuning to what matters. *Medical Education*, 48(1), pp. 44–52.

Fenwick, T. and Edwards, R. (2010). *Actor-network theory in education*. London: Routledge.

Fenwick, T., Edwards, R. and Sawchuk, P. (2011). *Emerging approaches to educational research: Tracing the socio-material*. Abingdon: Routledge.

Fenwick, T. and Nerland, M. (2014). *Reconceptualising professional learning: Sociomaterial knowledges, practices and responsibilities.* Abingdon: Routledge.

Fenwick, T. and Nimmo, G.R. (2015). Making visible what matters: Sociomaterial approaches for research and practice in healthcare education. In: J. Cleland and S.J. Durning, eds., *Researching medical education.* Chichester: John Wiley & Sons, pp. 67–80.

Gabbay, J., le May, A., Connell, C. and Klein, J.H. (2014). *Skilled for improvement? The improvement skills pyramid.* London: The Health Foundation. Available at: www.health.org.uk/sites/health/files/SkilledForImprovement_pyramindtemplate.pdf [Accessed 11 Nov. 2017].

Greenhalgh, T., Annandale, E., Ashcroft, R., Barlow, J., Black, N., Bleakley, A., Boaden, R., Braithwaite, J., Britten, N. and Carnevale, F. (2016). An open letter to The BMJ editors on qualitative research. *BMJ,* 352(i563).

Johnson, J. (1988). Mixing humans and nonhumans together: The sociology of a door-closer. *Social Problems,* 35(3), pp. 298–310.

Latour, B. (1999). On recalling ANT. In: J. Law and J. Hassard, eds., *Actor network theory and after.* Oxford: Blackwell Publishing, pp. 15–25.

Latour, B. (2005). *Reassembling the social: An introduction to actor-network-theory.* Oxford: Oxford University Press.

Latour, B. and Woolgar, S. (2013). *Laboratory life: The construction of scientific facts.* Princeton, NJ: Princeton University Press.

Law, J. (2004a). And if the global were small and noncoherent? Method, complexity, and the baroque. *Environment and Planning D: Society and Space,* 22(1), pp. 13–26.

Law, J. (2004b). *After method: Mess in social science research.* London: Routledge.

Law, J. (2006). Traduction/trahison: Notes on ANT. *Convergencia, UAEM, Mexico* (42), pp. 32–57.

Law, J. (2009). *'Collateral realities', version of 29th December 2009.* Available at: www.heterogeneities.net/publications/Law2009CollateralRealities.pdf [Accessed 11 Nov. 2017].

Lucas, B. and Nacer, H. (2015). *The habits of an improver: Thinking about learning for improvement in healthcare.* Discussion Paper. London: The Health Foundation.

McLean, C. and Hassard, J. (2004). Symmetrical absence/symmetrical absurdity: Critical notes on the production of actor-network accounts. *Journal of Management Studies,* 41(3), pp. 493–519.

McMurtry, A., Rohse, S. and Kilgour, K.N. (2016). Socio-material perspectives on inter-professional team and collaborative learning. *Medical Education,* 50(2), pp. 169–180.

Miettinen, R. (1999). The riddle of things: Activity theory and actor-network theory as approaches to studying innovations. *Mind, Culture, and Activity,* 6(3), pp. 170–195.

Mol, A. (1998). Ontological politics. A word and some questions. *The Sociological Review,* 46, pp. 74–89.

Mol, A. (2002). *The body multiple: Ontology in medical practice.* Durham: Duke University Press.

Mitchell, B. (2020). Student-led improvement science projects: A praxiographic, actor-network theory study. *Studies in Continuing Education,* 42(1), pp. 133–146.

Mitchell, B., Cristancho, S., Nyhof, B.B. and Lingard, L.A. (2017). Mobilising or standing still? A narrative review of Surgical Safety Checklist knowledge as developed in 25 highly cited papers from 2009 to 2016. *BMJ Quality & Safety,* 26(10).

Mulcahy, D. (2014). Re-thinking teacher professional learning: More than a representational account. In: T. Fenwick and M. Nerland, eds., *Reconceptualising professional learning: Sociomaterial knowledges, practices and responsibilities.* Abingdon: Routledge, pp. 52–66.

Nespor, J. (2014). *Knowledge in motion: Space, time and curriculum in undergraduate physics and management.* Abingdon: Routledge.

Paterson, G., Rossi, J., MacLean, S., Dolan, R., Johnston, T., Linden, D., Arbuckle, S., Lynch, N. and Davey, P. (2011). A patient safety 'student selected component' at the university of Dundee (UK). *International Journal of Clinical Skills*, 5(2).

Pels, D. (1996). The politics of symmetry. *Social Studies of Science*, 26(2), pp. 277–304.

Sørensen, E. (2009). *The materiality of learning: Technology and knowledge in educational practice*. Cambridge: Cambridge University Press.

Star, S.L. (1990). Power, technology and the phenomenology of conventions: On being allergic to onions. *The Sociological Review*, 38 (suppl 1), pp. 26–56.

Whitehead, C.R., Hodges, B.D. and Austin, Z. (2013). Dissecting the doctor: From character to characteristics in North American medical education. *Advances in Health Sciences Education*, 18(4), pp. 687–699.

Chapter 8

Reflections on the research

Following the example from Nespor's Knowledge in Motion, this chapter reflects on the research and the dilemmas encountered during data collection and analysis. It is hoped this will be useful for other researchers who are adopting an ANT sensibility. As there are no specific rules or frameworks, ANT as methodology necessarily remains fluid and dynamic. This chapter addresses the four issues with actor-networks mentioned in Chapter 4, and how these were addressed from a methodological perspective. This chapter also discusses what it means to 'cut the network' and 'follow the actor'. There are insights pertaining to the language of ANT, and how the research followed praxiography to address multiple worlds. I relate the five key points from my research to Adams and Thompson's (2016) set of heuristics as suggested approach to fieldwork. The empirical research is concluded with two personal stories.

ANT is an attractive theory to those of us who notice materials in practice. It is also an interesting theory in relation to education; the idea of learning as distributed, situated, assembled, provides an inspiring alternative to psychologised, individualised discourses that dominate learning in education. However, it is a bit more challenging when it comes to methodology and research. For example, how is it possible to avoid being representational, reductionist, and human-centred? How can we write about materials without claiming to represent or speak for them? How can we get the human out of the spotlight and resist the temptation to trace causality back to human action? The literature contends that ANT is a useful approach, but how do we 'do' it?

Networks as an analysis tool

To critique my analysis using networks, I returned to the four problems with actor-networks. In summary, networks can be conveyed as fixed; the researcher cannot perceive the network as an 'insider'; actor-network analysis has a tendency to represent only the most prominent actors; and there is a temptation to collapse everything into the network and not to exclude things which are not part of the network.

Dynamic networks

The types of networks I have been analysing are not physical networks of things with lines of connection in between. The 'narrative pathway' diagrams that helped me depict an actor did not accurately portray what I meant by a network, so this could be misleading for the reader. The diagrams portray a traditional, fixed, view of a network, rather than the dynamic actor–networks I was trying to illustrate. This is a dilemma similar to the one Nespor (2014) described when attempting to maintain movement in the data. I came to realise, throughout my analysis, that movement and dynamism were difficult to record and present in text and pictures, so I experimented with using images in different ways, such as the photomontages.

Describing networks as a researcher

My role as a researcher changed throughout the fieldwork as I became more familiar with the hospital environment and more comfortable around the students and staff. It was never my intention (and would have been incongruent with my ontological position) to attempt to be impartial or detached. I had to acknowledge that I would affect situations, and to be sensitive to the workplace environment and the needs of the students. In terms of sensitising to networks, I was not an outsider looking in, but neither was I a full participant. My changing position also influenced the effects I had on the networks I was studying, and I have tried to acknowledge this throughout the analysis by recording reflective notes. I wrote the following poem to describe my role as a researcher:

> I've joined the students for coffee and lunch;
> done some home baking, brought in mince pies;
> offered an ear, been asked my opinion;
> tried to placate;
> smiled and nodded, sympathised;
> sometimes succeeded, sometimes failed not to get involved;
> helped out and had a go;
> accepted a lift and the loan of a bus fare;
> held the books, collected things;
> kept my nose out, stuck my oar in;
> sat on the fence, went out on a limb;
> been reflexive, reflective, pragmatic, biased;
> been off the boil and on the ball;
> I've been present, manifestly absent and hidden all at once.

During the fieldwork, it was difficult to attend to relations and connections as these were only visible through effects: looking at 'things' themselves did not always show how they related and came together. For example, during an observation I noticed a nurse going to a set of filing cabinets in a corridor on the ward. She looked in one of the drawers and found that they had run out of that type of form, and so then started a set of practices to go and get some more forms. If the forms had been there, the nurse would have engaged in a different set of practices (continuing with her work). So, the absence of the form was agentic in that particular situation. Had I not been there at that particular time, I would not have noticed the role of the filing cabinets. The filing cabinets and the forms within the drawers were performing work that had become invisible.

> A nurse goes over to the filing drawers where forms are kept, complains that someone has gone off with the last one of a particular type so she has to restock.

Not just the 'big' actors

The analysis process I undertook was not systematic, as would be expected in other approaches. The advantages of being systematic are that a representative sample and the resulting analysis outputs can be generalised. The analysis I undertook was iterative, in that I looked at the detail of what I had recorded, but I was also able to consider the range of what I had collected. I achieved this by keeping hyperlinked records to each stage in the fieldwork and summaries with timelines. I also created annotated collages of each cohort to give me a sense of each SLISP. Although I had to be selective in what I focused on, I was able to keep stock of the breadth of what I had collected. In this way, I think I was able to acknowledge the detail of practice amongst the prominent actors.

Observing Cohort 2 and the sticker, it became evident that learning was not confined to individual students, and it was critical to have a theoretical sensitivity that allowed me to notice learning as a socio-material practice. The assemblage of materials changed over the month that I was with the students, influenced by both time and space. For example, there were time pressures for obtaining and making the sticker accessible. Buses and trains, the geographical distance of the two pharmacy students, the turnaround of staff on the ward and differing practices on the night shift all had an effect on when the stickers were needed. The location of equipment (the guillotine, printer, sticker paper) and the pharmacy offices, and access via buzzer system, shaped the SLISP as much as the forms and meetings. At the start of the project, the students were not attuned to the wards and the footfall of admissions (except perhaps the medical student, who had more experience, but could not have anticipated the low numbers of insulin-dependent patients; neither did the clinical lead). Because it was found that there was a small number of insulin-dependent patients on both wards during the time that the students were there for their project, that seemed to make it more important to 'catch' patients who were admitted during the night, and to perform activities such as 'simulated patient'. Over the space of the month, the clinicians on the ward began to become familiar with the sticker and seeing it on the medical reconciliation part of the form. In this example, knowledge was generated through assemblages coming together. For example, the colour pink was a signifier of medical forms relating to insulin, and the pink sticker became associated with other insulin paperwork.

There were other cases where I felt the network approach would not be appropriate. For example, one of the interviews was quite intense and left a lot of unanswered questions. ANT was not the right approach to draw out nuanced meanings. There was a lot of non-verbal communication in this interview that would be more suited to conversation analysis or psychologised approaches. In contrast, another interview I conducted was very practical and detailed, which proved useful for understanding existing networks, but it was difficult to get a sense of the specificities I needed for the SLISPs networks. Both interviews were still valuable to my research, but in different ways.

How to 'cut the network' and 'follow the actor'

The focus of my research was the SLISP, and I was interested in the associated networks; however, it was not always easy to disentangle the SLISP from other networks. The students from Cohort 2 completed the IHI Practicum templates such as PDSA cycles, run charts, process diagrams, and fishbone (cause-and-effect) diagram, so it was straightforward to include these visible artefacts as part of the SLISP. The medical student from Cohort 1 was undertaking a long-term project, still drawing from the same improvement science methodologies, but not adhering to the same IHI templates and format. They described the IHI forms as a 'mindset' rather than something to adhere rigidly to; it was therefore not possible for me to identify parts of the SLISP in Cohort 1 from the paperwork. The student from Cohort 1's improvement work was also involved in activities in specialist groups and to existing knowledge of medical practices. In ANT terms, it could be said that there were existing networks relating to antibiotic prescription improvement and that the student's activities reinforced of some of these. Attuning to the SLISP networks was a challenging task, so I drew from the idea of using the gentamycin form as an actor to follow through my fieldnotes. This allowed me to identify points of translation, and forces and effects. Through observations and interviews, the SLISP gentamycin network emerged as part of other, overlapping networks. These included the gentamycin prescribing network, antimicrobial networks, and other prescribing and recording networks. The forces within the SLISP included clinical staff and the antimicrobial prescribing groups. It was difficult, as a researcher, to know where to 'cut the network'. For example, I could have included government targets relating to Hospital Acquired Infections, antimicrobial stewardship training and antimicrobial resistance agendas, as these created forces and tensions. However, these appeared to be distant and connected with other, closer networks in several places. It seemed more appropriate to focus on specific clinical staff as a more proximate force in the SLISP network.

As I became aware of the strength of connections, it became clearer where to cut the network.

It was difficult not to pull everything I observed into the networks I conceptualised. In a way, everything appeared to be connected. To counteract this, I attended to the effects and forces in the networks; if forces and effects were weak, this could signal where to cut the network. However, I had to judge whether the effect was weak or whether there was something I had not observed or encountered in an interview. I did not look at inequalities or gender issues in my study as this was not my focus. I also did not look at the wider medical student community, even though this might have been useful for understanding wider educational issues. There were some instances where I would have liked to have explored this further, but I had to 'cut the network'; I constantly referred back to research questions to help me do this. I did not include patients in my research. The students did not either, although some checking was done with patients along the way. Mostly the students were looking at forms and how they had been filled in. They recorded information from the forms onto their own data collection forms. The numbers represented patient readings, but not the patients themselves.

Researching symmetry

My research addressed symmetry directly using observation and visual analysis. Although there were interviews with humans, the purpose was to draw out unseen connections, forces and associations. Adams and Thompson's (2016) set of heuristics for post-human inquiry in their book *Research in a Posthuman World: Interviews with digital objects*, addresses many of the critiques aimed at ANT and symmetry. The key points made in the last chapter align with these heuristics, which is encouraging in the sense of ANT as an enduring and cohesive approach. The following points first mention each heuristic in italics and go on to describe how these resonated with my study.

The first four points relate to attending to things. *Gathering anecdotes*: I referred to stories in my methodology that ran through my data and developed these through description to construct three, robust anecdotes. These started out as smaller stories assembled after the data were collected. Some stories fell short of an anecdote because of fewer connections and strength than other stories. For example, I started to describe the story of the guillotine in detail as part of the sticker network, but the description did not carry as far as I thought it would. I therefore integrated this detail into the sticker anecdote. *Following the actors*: To begin analysis, my first strategy was to identify actors. As discussed earlier in this chapter, I needed to ensure that I was not privileging big or important actors, as their presence would induce the absence of other actors. As described with the guillotine, some actors had more connections with networks than others, but to notice this, I had to follow them. *Listening for the invitational quality of things*: my second key point is about materials inviting (and excluding) practice. The interviews were helpful for understanding some of the less noticeable connections, and there were some surprises with incidents during observations. There were two examples of note: the invisible drawer and the secret drawer. Both highlighted how materials shape practice, and both were enacted as taken-for-granted practices, which may have been overlooked. *Studying breakdowns, accidents, and anomalies:* in my research I attended to invisible practices such as the buzzer and bleep systems. This relates to how materials shape practice, and also how mundane processes become black-boxed or treated as matters of fact.

The last two points relate to analysing materialites. *Discovering the spectrum of human-technology-world relations:* my fifth point is about assembling realities and relates to the questions put forward for this heuristic in terms of human-technology-world relations. *Unravelling translations:* this relates to the ontological politics of learning, my fourth point. This refers to how work is ordered and assembled and how different realities are enacted, including collateral realities.

Describing multiple worlds

As I progressed with the research there were facets of multiple worlds that began to unfold for me. I had started with a praxiographic approach which helped me to notice difference, ambivalence, and ambiguity in the data. This, for me, is where the advantage of ANT as non-representative becomes evident: if I had sought for generalisation, or to claim that my research was representative of the sample, then difference might have been treated as 'outlier', 'atypical' or 'confounder'. At the end of The Body Multiple, Mol (2002, p. 152) observes:

> Shifting from understanding objects as the focus point of various perspectives to following them as they are enacted in a variety of practices implies a shift from asking how sciences represent to asking how they intervene.

ANT enabled me to follow and unfold difference rather than try to smooth it over or to explain the phenomenon in the context of patterns that I had drawn out. Applying the ANT methodology to this process, I could say that this was a method assemblage, taking into account that when something was made visible then something else might be made absent or other. I could also say that creating a meta-narrative would involve regulating difference in my own research. It is therefore appropriate that I did not follow a conventional analysis process for qualitative research of thematic analysis and coding. Although some degree of organisation and selection was involved, I tried to do this through sensitising to the data and visual analysis, creating descriptions and anecdotes.

My first anecdote exploring multiple worlds was the measurement of 'duration'. I noticed this because the student encountered difficulties in recording a yes/no answer regarding whether or not it had been recorded, and it had appeared very straightforward at first. It took a long time to draw out descriptions from the data to describe why recording duration was so complex; at one point, my supervisor said that they were not convinced that this was an example of a multiplicity. It required further description to present duration as a multiplicity, and a turning point came in an example in the data which demonstrated how practices appear to 'peel away' from each other into multiple worlds. It was unnerving to continue apply work and effort when there was a risk that nothing convincing would emerge, but this is the work of an ANT analyst: you have to hold your nerve. Law (2009, p. 15), for example, explains how he explored non-coherence when studying a conference talk:

> In practice, practices are always more or less non-coherent. They work by enacting different versions of reality and more or less successfully holding these together. But if there is multiplicity rather than singularity then we have an entry point. If we look for non-coherences within practices we will find them. We will discover collateral realities. And, this is the move to an ontological politics, we may take sides and hope to make a difference. Reality is no longer destiny.

At the end of my research, there were two incidents that indicated not coherence but perhaps affinity or serendipity with ANT. The first was rather esoteric but felt significant to my role as an ANT researcher. The second is encouraging for future research.

Story one

I was in an airport and I picked up a book: *Labyrinths* by Borges (1964). I flicked through the pages and happened upon a story entitled Avatars of the Tortoise. I was drawn to the story, bought the book, and sat and read it straight away. The story included a description of Zeno's paradox related to a race between Achilles and a tortoise: the philosophical argument was that, if the tortoise started first, Achilles would never catch him up because of diminishing returns, fracturing time, and distance into an impossible infinity. When I read this I thought of ANT, of how complexity is unfolded, un-black-boxed, ad infinitum. When I returned home, I re-read some of the chapters from Latour's (2005) Reassembling the Social, and there was Zeno. Latour described the same thing I had been thinking. Perhaps I had retained the name from my first reading; perhaps this was a coincidence; or perhaps we were thinking along the same lines.

Story two

Adams and Thompson's (2016) book *Researching a Posthuman World: Interviews with digital objects* came out in 2016, and I had avoided reading this straight away as I had already started my analysis. Instead, I finished writing my five key points and then read the book. As I read through the heuristics, I found that many of these resonated with my own study. As I described earlier in this chapter, my five key points easily nestled in some of the heuristics, and it would not be difficult for a future study to start with the heuristics. I felt encouraged by this, again, as though I had returned.

Perhaps these stories describe the finish point as inevitable as a ball rolling down a hill; it will stop at the bottom, in a different place to where it started. Or perhaps it was like getting lost and coming back to the same point, but everything else has changed. Either way, it has been an interesting journey.

References

Adams, C. and Thompson, T.L. (2016). *Researching a posthuman world: Interviews with digital objects*. London: Palgrave Macmillan.

Borges, J.L. (1964). *Labyrinths: Selected stories & other writings*. London: New Directions Publishing.

Latour, B. (2005). *Reassembling the social: An introduction to actor-network-theory*. Oxford: Oxford University Press.

Law, J. (2009). *'Collateral realities', version of 29th December 2009*. Available at: www.heteroge neities.net/publications/Law2009CollateralRealities.pdf [Accessed 11 Nov. 2017].

Mol, A. (2002). *The body multiple: Ontology in medical practice*. Durham: Duke University Press.

Nespor, J. (2014). *Knowledge in motion: Space, time and curriculum in undergraduate physics and management*. Abingdon: Routledge.

Index

Note: Page numbers in *italics* indicate a figure on the corresponding page.

Printed in the United States
by Baker & Taylor Publisher Services